Caring Enough to Lead

THIRD EDITION

For all those "carpenters by trade" who are transforming America's
schools through their courage, caring, and commitment.

Builders and Wreckers

I watched them tearing a building down,

A gang of men in a busy town.

With a ho, heave, ho and a lusty yell

They swung a beam and a wall fell.

I asked the foreman, "Are these men skilled?

Like the men you'd hire if you had to build?"

He laughed as he replied, "No, indeed.

Just common labor is all I need.

I can easily wreck in a day or two

What builders have taken years to do."

I asked myself as I went away,

Which of these roles have I tried to play?

Am I a builder who works with care

Measuring life by rule and square?

Or am I a wrecker who walks the town

Content with the labor of tearing down?

—Author unknown

Caring Enough to Lead

THIRD EDITION

How Reflective Practice Leads to Moral Leadership

Leonard O. Pellicer
Foreword by Terrence E. Deal

CORWIN PRESS
A SAGE Publications Company
Thousand Oaks, CA 91320

For information:

Corwin Press
A Sage Publications Company
2455 Teller Road
Thousand Oaks, California 91320
www.corwinpress.com

Sage Publications India Pvt. Ltd.
B 1/I 1 Mohan Cooperative Industrial Area
Mathura Road, New Delhi 110 044
India

Sage Publications Ltd.
1 Oliver's Yard
55 City Road
London EC1Y 1SP
United Kingdom

Sage Publications Asia-Pacific Pte. Ltd.
33 Pekin Street #02–01
Far East Square
Singapore 048763

Printed in the United States of America

Library of Congress Cataloging-in-Publication Data

Pellicer, Leonard O.
Caring enough to lead: How reflective practice leads to moral leadership/Leonard O. Pellicer—3rd ed.
    p. cm.
Includes bibliographical references and index.
ISBN 978-1-4129-5597-3 (cloth)
ISBN 978-1-4129-5598-0 (pbk.)
1. Educational leadership—United States. 2. School management and organization—United States. 3. School principals—United States. 4. School administrators—United States. I. Title.

LB2805.P375 2008
371.2—dc22
                                            2007011195
This book is printed on acid-free paper.

            11   10   9   8   7   6   5   4   3

Acquisitions Editor:	Elizabeth Brenkus
Editorial Assistants:	Desirée Enayati and Ena Rosen
Production Editor:	Melanie Birdsall
Typesetter:	C&M Digitals (P) Ltd.
Copy Editor:	Alison Hope
Proofreader:	Gail Fay
Indexer:	Michael Ferreira
Cover Designer:	Rose Storey
Graphic Designer:	Scott Van Atta

CONTENTS

Foreword to the Third Edition   vii
Terrence E. Deal

Foreword to the Second Edition   ix
Governor Richard W. Riley

Foreword to the First Edition   xi
Aretha B. Pigford

Preface   xiii

Acknowledgments   xix

About the Author   xxi

1. It's Better to Know Some of the Questions   1
    Than All of the Answers

2. Why Am I Going to Visit Bob?   6

3. What Is a Leader?   11

4. Why Should Leaders Care About Caring?   24

5. What Do I Care About?   35

6. What Do I Believe About People?   43

7. Am I Taking Care of My Water Buffalo?   53

8. What Does It Mean to Be a Teacher?   58

9. Am I Willing to Share Power?   64

10. What Does It Mean to Be Responsible?   72

11. Why Am I Doing This?   80

12. Am I Willing to Jump for the Trapeze?   87

13. Who's the King or Queen of the Jungle?   94

14. "Honey, Do These Pants Make Me Look Fat?"   99

15. Can I Care Enough to Do the Little Things?   105

16. "Can You Just Call Me Willie, Mrs. Peterson?"   113

17. How Are Schools Transformed?   120

18. Why Do I Choose to Lead?   130

19. What Do Leaders Owe to Those Who Follow?   136

20. Can I Care Enough to Be My Own Best Friend?   144

21. Will That Be a Senior Cup of Coffee?   151

22. Your Leadership Becomes You!   160

References   **170**

Index   **173**

FOREWORD TO THE
THIRD EDITION

B efore he passed away in 2005, Peter Drucker made an apt but contro-
versial statement: "Everything you have learned is wrong." He was
talking about leadership, and his remarks were right on target. We've heard
a version of what he said before. Robert McNamara, architect of our
approach to war in Vietnam, admitted in retrospect, "We were wrong, terribly wrong." Taken together, these two quotes reveal the futile path we have
taken in our quest to understand and apply the lessons of leadership. Here is
a book that has it right.

Leonard Pellicer is more believable than many authors because he practices what he preaches. As Dr. Peggy Redman (also my cousin), one of his
colleagues at the University of La Verne, observes, "In my initial meeting
with Leonard, I was amazed at how perceptive he was. He radiates caring in
dealing with both people and tough issues. It doesn't make any difference
where you are in the formal pecking order. He deals with the custodian or the
president with the same authentic touch. He's made a big difference here."

The book is a blend of book knowledge and street smarts. Wisdom always
trumps knowledge when leaders struggle to do the right things rather than
search for recipes for doing things the right way. None of us exists in a world
where everything is clear-cut. That's why managers rarely become leaders.
Managers have a solution, but figuring out the problem in a messy, senseless
situation eludes the boundaries of rational thinking. Ron Heifetz categorizes
problems into three classifications. Type 1 problems are straightforward. Both
the problem and solution are known quantities. Type 2 problems portray those
challenges where the problem is well defined but the solution is hard to pin
down. Type 3 problems present a conundrum: both the problem and the solution are obscure. Managers excel with Type 1 issues and do reasonably well
with Type 2 issues. But it takes real leaders to wrestle with Type 3 issues.

Human organizations are fraught with ambiguity, which is why leadership is so crucial.

From this, it follows that leaders must first come to know themselves. That inner journey is a dominant theme in this book. Leadership is inextricably tied with the heart and soul of leaders. But that's only the bud. Flowering comes through the layers of experience. There is no guide for how to become a leader. One is always becoming a leader through the hard knocks of leading. Leaders need the courage to chart a promising course over unknown and treacherous territory. Errors abound. But muddling through with trial and error, good leaders find a path. If you stay on the highway you probably will arrive at a predetermined destination. Venturing on your own may blaze a trail for others to follow.

One of this book's highlights is that Pellicer exposes himself. He bares his soul, which encourages self-reflection on the part of the reader. He identifies the emulation of role models as one of the valuable lessons in learning to lead. In making himself so vulnerable and accessible he becomes what he advocates—an exemplar of the virtues of caring. In *Hero of a Thousand Faces*, Joseph Campbell describes the epic journey of the hero who enters the darkness of the unknown, survives, and then returns to bestow (in his words) boons on those who have not yet ventured out. The fundamental joy of leadership is giving gifts to others. That is precisely what this book represents— a gift from someone who shows us that leading and caring go hand in hand. I have skimmed through all too many books on leadership. Most don't speak to me. This one got my attention. Through a rich collection of anecdotes and stories, rather than pronouncements and recipes, I know it will grab yours.

—Terrence E. Deal

FOREWORD TO THE SECOND EDITION

As governor of South Carolina in the 1980s, and then as U.S. secretary of education in the 1990s, I had the great fortune to be a leader in education. Imagine the overwhelming feeling of making decisions that would affect all children of a state or of our great nation. What, then, are the characteristics of leadership that could best serve a person facing this heavy responsibility? Well, it isn't a feeling of power and importance. It isn't even experience, though knowledge of the subject is important. And it certainly isn't the self-confidence to give orders to your employees, expecting or demanding that they be carried out. No, it's more than all of that, and that is what my friend Leonard Pellicer understands and shares with us in this second edition of his book, *Caring Enough to Lead*. I first knew Leonard as an outstanding principal of a high school in my home school district. His reputation as a special kind of school leader had already been established. He was about the work of "being" a school leader. He worked in the area of staff development for teachers and administrators in Florida; he was a Fulbright Scholar, training school leaders in the Philippines; and he continued his education leadership teaching postsecondary educators.

Caring Enough to Lead is based on Leonard Pellicer's three-plus decades of varied experience as a professional educator. He has not only served, but he has observed and listened and recorded what he has learned.

Yes, he has learned the importance of education as a building block for our democracy and as the key building block for every child's future. He believes in the power of education for human and societal development. And he cares enough to fight for his beliefs.

Here again, he is sharing his conviction about leadership with us in a very personal and practical way: he is sharing his touching story about his visits with his friend who struggled with Alzheimer's disease, his observations about the rhythms of the farmer in the Philippines leading and guiding the powerful water buffalo, the difficulty of making tough choices when asked by a woman if "these pants make me look too fat"—that is, he is sharing his views on truth versus sensitivity to one's feelings. All these stories approach the subject of leadership in a creative and interesting way.

One of the most revealing stories is about transforming a low-performing school. Zenia Elementary School was such a school until it gained a caring principal who had a simple but powerful vision: no child will fail. The principal built a staff and entire school community that shared that vision. He cared enough to lead, and it made a real difference in the lives of all children fortunate enough to attend Zenia Elementary School.

In order to help the reader internalize his message, the author has included a set of reflective exercises at the end of each chapter. These exercises help readers realize that, indeed, they are the ones to whom the book speaks. And by applying these ideas to one's own involvement in education and one's own life, you can begin "dancing the dance of a leader" who cares enough to lead.

—Governor Richard W. Riley

FOREWORD TO THE
FIRST EDITION

A few years ago, I received an incredible gift: the opportunity to partici-pate in a leadership development program sponsored by the Kellogg Foundation. This three-year experience allowed me to visit cultures throughout the world and explore leadership firsthand. My explorations took me to a quaint Amish community in Pennsylvania, to a dirt-poor sugarcane plantation in Costa Rica, to a cramped township in South Africa, to a condemned public housing project in Houston, and to an opulent presidential palace in Central America. During my journey, I observed the leadership of the rich and powerful as well as the poor and victimized. I met with internationally acclaimed Nobel Peace Prize recipients, with impoverished Chiapa women weavers, with embittered South African students, and with grief-stricken Guatemalan mothers. My mis-sion was simple: to observe and analyze leadership and attempt to reach some conclusions about this elusive phenomenon. As I began my journey, I did so acknowledging that the study of leadership was nothing new to me. As a former graduate student in educational administration, I was steeped in leadership theory. As a professor of educational administration, I had spent more than ten years teaching leadership classes. As a former principal, assistant dean, and associate superintendent, I had numerous opportunities to practice leadership. But this journey took me down a new path, a path that challenged me to see leadership from a different perspective, a path that shifted my focus from the "behaviors" to the "being" of leadership.

By the end of my journey, I had reached several conclusions, the most definitive of which was simple, but profound: authentic leaders are people who do what they do because of a genuine desire to make things better for others. The fact that a personal sacrifice might be required does not stop them. Simply stated, they care enough to lead. Caring enough—that is the primary motivation for authentic leadership as well as the essential message of this book. Filled with anecdotes and vignettes, *Caring Enough to Lead* provides a powerful account of Leonard Pellicer's personal journey into leadership. Through a series of intriguing, insightful questions, Leonard challenges us to take an introspective, reflective journey into ourselves, the first step toward becoming an authentic leader. Unlike the typical book on leadership, *Caring* is not about doing: There are no checklists of behaviors. It is about being.

The author is eminently qualified to write about leadership, not because of his impressive academic credentials, but because of his life experiences and his unique ability to create meaning from them. Whether by choice or by circumstance, Leonard's life has been characterized by being out front. Throughout his life, in a great variety of formal and informal leadership roles, he has continued to inspire a host of willing followers. Why are persons so willing to follow him? During our twenty-year association, I have observed the following: First, he regards leadership as a sacred trust given to him by willing followers. He respects and honors that trust. Second, he listens to all the voices and, when necessary, gives voice to those who are silent or marginalized. Third, he is not afraid to push the limits and inspires those who fear leaving the security of their comfort zones to do likewise. Most important, he understands fully that leadership is about service—not about power.

Caring Enough to Lead is Leonard's personal gift to us. In it, he lets his guard down and allows us to observe him as he takes inventory of himself, with the hope that we will be challenged to do likewise. It is only by doing so that each of us can begin the journey to authentic leadership.

—*Aretha B. Pigford*

PREFACE

No one who takes the time to read *Caring Enough to Lead* will mistake it for a textbook. Rather than a rehash of the tenets of leadership according to a host of theoreticians past and present, this book presents a highly personal perspective on what it means to care enough to be an effective leader. This book is not the least bit concerned with leadership theory and the organizational structures, processes, and rational technical skills that flow from it, but rather is concerned with an understanding of who we are as leaders and what we can become as we bond with others in meaningful ways to help transform schools. So if it's more theory that you are seeking, this is definitely not the book for you!

The discussion of leaders and leadership is thousands of years old. As far as we can tell, men, women, and even children have been leading for as long as human beings have banded together and worked cooperatively, initially in an effort to survive and later also to improve the quality of life. Countless studies have been conducted over many years in efforts to determine what causes or allows some people to lead and others to follow. Our perspectives on leadership have matured a great deal over the last century. Although much has been learned about leaders and leading, for the most part leadership remains an intriguing mystery.

Through an arduous process marked by careful study and keen observation, we have progressed all the way from the belief that leaders are born, not made, to embracing the notion that leaders must connect with others in an organization in such a way that the organization becomes a reflection of a set of powerful common core values that can serve to raise the organization to a higher moral and ethical level. That's quite a journey by any stretch of the imagination.

Some popular book titles published throughout the 1990s and beyond illustrate a growing fascination with a softer side of leadership—what some might term ethical or moral leadership. *Managing From the Heart* (Bracey, Rosenblum, Sanford, & Trueblood, 1990), *Moral Leadership: Getting to the*

Heart of School Improvement (Sergiovanni, 1992), *Stewardship: Choosing Service Over Self-Interest* (Block, 1993), *Leading With Soul: An Uncommon Journey of Spirit* (Bolman & Deal, 1995), *The Loyalty Effect* (Reichheld, 1996), *On Becoming a Servant Leader* (Greenleaf, 1996), *Managing by Values* (Blanchard & O'Connor, 1997), *Leadership From the Inside Out* (Cashman, 1998), and *The Servant Leader* (Blanchard & Hodges, 2003) are illustrative of this trend toward moral leadership.

Caring Enough to Lead is this writer's humble attempt to expand the discussion of leadership beyond what it means to perform in a leadership role in order to get at what it really means to be a leader. As Sergiovanni (1992) has put it,

> The management values now considered legitimate are biased toward rationality, logic, objectivity, the importance of self-interest, explicitness, individuality, and detachment. Emphasizing these values causes us to neglect emotions, the importance of group membership, sense and meaning, morality, self-sacrifice, duty, and obligation as additional values. Furthermore, the bases of authority for today's leadership practice rely heavily on bureaucracy, psychological knowledge or skill, and the technical rationality that emerges from theory and research. Emphasizing those three bases causes us to neglect professional and moral authority as additional bases for leadership practice. (p. xiii)

In the simplest of terms, this book is not concerned with what leaders say, know, or are able to do. All these elements of leadership have been dealt with sufficiently in the past. *Caring Enough to Lead* is about being a leader. I firmly believe that Sergiovanni (1992) is correct in his contention that we have viewed leadership from a very narrow perspective in the past. In doing so, we may have negated what could be the most important aspects of what it means to be a leader, the so-called moral dimension of leadership. *Caring Enough to Lead* is a deliberate attempt to understand and expand some of the yet unexplored and heretofore unexplained dimensions of moral leadership.

INTENDED AUDIENCE

Caring Enough to Lead has several intended audiences. This book is not exclusively for people in formal leadership roles, but for all those who feel a deeply personal responsibility to provide the most caring, compassionate, and effective leadership they can in whatever leadership roles they may find themselves serving. Therefore, the content of this book is appropriate for a broad range of formal and informal leaders in educational institutions, business and industry, social service agencies, government service, the military, and just about any other leadership role where someone is committed to being the best leader he or she can be while serving others in a compassionate and caring way. The book is intended for both practicing leaders and those who are in the process of preparing to become leaders. My hope in writing *Caring Enough to Lead* is to help those with leadership responsibilities understand that leading is concerned much more with being than it is with doing, and that caring is at the very heart of being.

UNIQUE FEATURES OF THE BOOK

The content of this book is based on my more than thirty-five years of studying leadership while serving in a variety of leadership roles. The fundamental truths that are the foundation of this discussion of leadership are based on both real-life experiences and expert opinion. The majority of the chapter titles are in the form of questions, and many additional questions are included in the narrative to help the reader focus on what I believe to be the most fundamental elements of successful leadership (e.g., What do I care about? What do I believe about people?). Scenarios, metaphors, and vignettes are used to illustrate key points and make the reading of the book an enjoyable as well as an enlightening personal experience rather than just another boring academic exercise. A special feature of *Caring Enough to Lead* is the inclusion of an expanded set of reflective exercises at the end of each chapter. These exercises encourage readers to step back and examine in a personal way who they are as leaders and human beings and who they might want to become. By completing these reflective exercises, readers can, in effect, produce personal journals documenting where they are on their individual journeys to becoming the kind of people and leaders that they ultimately want to become.

NEED FOR THE BOOK

In 1999, I wrote a book for school leaders about the importance of caring to effective school leadership. That book, *Caring Enough to Lead: Leadership and the Sacred Trust,* was well received by school leaders and was subsequently republished in a second edition. Although these first two books were written expressly for educational leaders, over the years I have received considerable feedback from leaders in other fields—from business and industry, to the military, to government service, and even to the legal profession. These leaders have read one or the other of these first two editions suggesting that the content is appropriate and needed by leaders in all fields. It is my belief that good leaders from all fields should be interested in sharing information and ideas with each other. So although this third edition is still aimed principally at school leaders, I sincerely hope that through this book I am able to contribute something to the discussion of leadership to my colleagues from many walks of life.

I am convinced that there is a lack of caring leadership in many of our organizations today, resulting in low engagement in their work by a significant majority of American workers across all fields. Low engagement in the workplace translates into many serious problems, including an absence of commitment by employees to the mission of the organization, poor-quality work, absenteeism, high employee turnover, low morale, and eventually declining productivity and the loss of competitiveness. Unfortunately, the problems resulting from the lack of caring leadership are not problems that can be solved with the head—they are problems that must be solved with the heart. This book is written for those leaders who have the heart to care enough to lead. It is especially for those who want to solve what I am convinced is the most fundamental problem afflicting many organizations today: the lack of caring leadership.

SCOPE AND TREATMENT

Caring Enough to Lead is a collection of ideas and understandings; it is not a how-to manual. The chapters, which are relatively brief, illustrate important concepts of leadership through a series of questions, vignettes, selected quotations, and personal stories. Although the first and last chapters need to appear in that order, most of the others could easily be placed at random because they are self-contained and complete. Below are brief descriptions of the contents of several selected chapters, and of chapters that are new to this book to illustrate the uniqueness of the book.

Chapter 1, It's Better to Know Some of the Questions Than All of the Answers, sets the stage for the chapters that follow. The essence of this chapter is that questions are more important than answers for leaders because life's essential questions are eternal, whereas answers to questions frequently vary with the time, circumstances, and personalities. Because questions are more important than answers for leaders, the remainder of the book suggests some of the essential questions that leaders should be asking and answering for themselves if they hope to become the leaders that they ultimately would like to become.

Chapter 4, Why Should Leaders Care About Caring? is a new chapter in this edition that was written especially for those leaders whose chief concern is the bottom line—that is, those who feel an obligation to focus on the dollars and cents aspects of leadership. This chapter provides some solid evidence as to why it makes good business sense for leaders in all fields of endeavor to care about caring.

Chapter 5, What Do I Care About? illustrates that the essential things that a person cares about determine to a great extent who that person is as a human being and as a leader. The question, "What do I care about?" is critical for leaders, because the things that people value most highly dictate what they will be passionate about, fight for, sacrifice for, and in some cases, what they may even give their lives for. What leaders care about and how that caring is manifested will also ultimately determine whether or not others can and will trust them enough to allow them to lead.

Chapter 7, Am I Taking Care of My Water Buffalo? is concerned with the role that cooperation and mutual respect can play in successful leadership. The story of a farmer and a water buffalo plowing a rice paddy together is used to illustrate how much we need each other to accomplish any goal. The point is made that, although there are many different roles to play in any organization, every role is critical to the success or failure of the organization.

Chapter 19, What Do Leaders Owe to Those Who Follow? is also new to this edition and explores the nature of the debt that leaders owe followers. While most of us are very aware of the rewards of leadership, we sometimes forget that there are significant debts that go hand-in-hand with the privileges of leading.

Chapter 22, Your Leadership Becomes You! is the final chapter in the book and describes the personal metamorphosis that one must experience in order to ultimately become the leader that he or she wishes to become. This final chapter offers a series of suggested steps one can take to become a caring leader, and emphasizes once again that effective leadership is not about knowing, saying, or doing things in a leadership role. Rather, effective leadership is all about being something.

ACKNOWLEDGMENTS

There have been precious few times in my life when I have been afforded an opportunity to write something that I genuinely wanted to write. This book has clearly been that exception that all writers covet. I am eternally grateful to Corwin Press for giving me that opportunity—not just once, but three times!

Lizzie, I genuinely appreciate the opportunity I was afforded to work with you as my editor. No editor could have been more patient, encouraging, helpful, and professional. Thank you for being so responsive to my inquiries, and so thoughtful and considerate while weighing my proposals. Over the brief period that we have worked together, I have come to respect and admire your knowledge, skill, and commitment to a high standard of excellence.

I also want to express my appreciation to two other key players on the Corwin Press editorial team, Melanie Birdsall, my production editor, and Alison Hope, my copy editor. Thank you, Melanie, for managing the production process so flawlessly. Alison, you helped me say what I wanted and needed to say so much better than I could have otherwise. Are you available to help me argue with my wife?

To all those who read drafts and offered advice during the writing of several editions of this book, your contributions as reviewers are gratefully acknowledged. You really told me what I needed to hear and nothing could be more caring than that. Susan Fortune, I truly regret that you left this life too soon and didn't get the opportunity to review this latest draft. Thank you, Donna, Diane, and Ron for the many ways that you helped and supported me throughout the project. To my graduate students Chris, Ginny, Thelma, Phyllis, and Megan, who made all those trips to the library, checked references for me, and helped me find stuff when I lost it, Thank you! Thank you! Thank you!

To my chief role models in leadership, Aretha, Barbara, Ken, Martha, Peggy, Ron, Rudolph, and Tom, thank you for demonstrating through your caring leadership and friendship what it truly means to be a leader and a friend. To all my colleagues with whom I have worked in public school districts as well as those at the University of South Carolina and the University of La Verne, words can't begin to express what an honor and a privilege it has been for me to have been a part of such dedicated and caring groups of educational leaders for most of my professional life.

A very special thank you to my cherished sons, Patrick and Christopher, for teaching me humility and reminding me frequently that I don't control very much in my own life and even less in yours. I am so very proud of the thoughtful, kind, and caring people you have both become. Finally, to my beautiful, caring, and talented wife, Nancy, thank you for your steadfast love and support over more than forty years. No one has ever been blessed with a more wonderful life partner.

PUBLISHER'S ACKNOWLEDGMENTS

Corwin Press gratefully acknowledges the contributions of the following individuals:

Steve Bounds, Assistant Professor
Henderson State University
Arkadelphia, AR

Kristine Servais, Assistant Professor
North Central College
Naperville, IL

Karen L. Tichy, Associate Superintendent for Instruction
Catholic Education Office
St. Louis, MO

Michelle L. Tichy, Assistant Professor
St. Norbert College
De Pere, WI

Richard Yee, Principal
Oster Elementary School
San José, CA

Rosemarie Young, Principal
Watson Lane Elementary School
Louisville, KY

Steve Zsiray, Principal and CEO
InTech Collegiate High School
North Logan, UT

ABOUT THE AUTHOR

Leonard O. Pellicer retired July 1, 2007, after serving seven years as the first dean of the College of Education and Organizational Leadership at the University of La Verne, in La Verne, California. Prior to his work at La Verne University, he served on the faculty at the University of South Carolina for twenty-two years, and was named Distinguished Professor Emeritus when he left that university in June 2000.

During a career spanning more than thirty-five years, he served in a number of teaching and leadership roles. He served as the first director of the South Carolina Educational Policy Center at the University of South Carolina, where he was also the director of the African American Professors Program, a program designed to address the problem of a shortage of African American professors at predominantly white higher-education institutions.

His experiences prior to joining the faculty at the University of South Carolina include service as a high school and middle school teacher, high school assistant principal, high school principal, and director of a teacher education center that provided staff development opportunities for teachers and administrators in five Florida school districts. From 1986 to 1987, he was a Fulbright Scholar in Southeast Asia. During this period, he taught graduate classes at the University of the Philippines, and used his expertise in school leadership to assist in developing programs to train school leaders in the region. From 1992 to 1995, he spent a good deal of time in the Republic of South Africa as a member of a team that developed a field-based training program for black principals in the new South Africa. He holds a bachelor's degree in English education, and master's and doctoral degrees in educational administration from the University of Florida in Gainesville. For more than twenty-five years, he has written, consulted, and spoken extensively in the areas of school leadership, instructional leadership, and educational programs for disadvantaged students. He has written or cowritten more than sixty books, book chapters, journal articles, and monographs, including two books with Lorin Anderson for Corwin Press: *A Handbook for Teacher Leaders* (1995) and *Teacher Peer Assistance and Review: A Practical Guide for Teachers and Administrators* (2001).

CHAPTER ONE

IT'S BETTER TO KNOW SOME OF THE QUESTIONS THAN ALL OF THE ANSWERS

B ack in the days when I was fortunate enough to have a lawn, I enjoyed mowing my grass on Saturday mornings. I'm not sure why this was such a pleasurable experience for me, but it really and truly was something I looked forward to doing. One of the things I enjoyed most was the smell of the newly mowed grass; another was the feeling of accomplishment that comes with completing a project that allows you to admire the results of your labor instantly. Those of us who have been educators never tire of experiences such as this, experiences that provide even a small measure of instant gratification. Maybe this is because it seems as if we have to wait most of a lifetime to see the results of our efforts with children in classrooms.

Although I like smelling the newly mowed grass and admiring the results of my handiwork, perhaps the thing I liked best about mowing my grass was the feeling of power I derived from mowing down all those thousands and thousands of blades of grass while gliding along effortlessly behind my almost new, self-propelled Honda mower. When I first brought my Honda mower home from the store, my wife took one look at it and exclaimed, "Wow! It looks like you could drive it to town." My wife doesn't exaggerate—it was an impressive mower!

Over the years, I established a pattern for mowing my grass that suited me perfectly. I always attacked the project by cutting all the odd-shaped, uneven areas around the edges of my lawn first, so that after a while I was left with a large circle of uncut grass in the middle of the yard. Then I would go round and round the remaining circle of grass in a nice easy rhythm interrupted only by my stopping occasionally to empty the bulging grass bag. It was downright peaceful and highly gratifying!

As I cruised along effortlessly, watching the circle grow smaller and smaller with each completed circuit, I would wear my genuine Dale Earnhardt earphones and listen to public radio. There were, and are, a lot of good shows on PBS radio on Saturday mornings. There was *Rabbit Ears Radio,* and there's *Car Talk* and my favorite mowing show, *Whad'Ya Know?* which is produced by Public Radio International and is broadcast live. The host of the show is the clever and entertaining Michael Feldman. Michael always begins the show with a question for his audience. "Whad'ya know?" he asks in a rather loud and demanding voice, to which the members of the studio audience (and all of us listening out there in radio land) reply in unison, "Not much!"

The show is a quiz show, and as it progresses, it becomes more and more evident that indeed, the contestants on the show don't know much. At least they don't know very much about the questions that Michael Feldman has for them. The questions on the show are designed to trip up the contestants and make them look foolish by asking about silly and often obscure facts gleaned from nonsensical categories such as "things you should have learned in school had you been paying attention." The producers of *Whad'Ya Know?* acknowledge that the questions are a little ridiculous, with a disclaimer that advises listeners to get their own shows if they don't like the questions they use.

Thirty or forty years ago, had you asked me "whad'ya know?" I would have responded very differently to the question than I would today. Like many young people (including the two sons who grew up in my house over the past several decades), I thought I knew just about everything in this world that I needed to know.

It was during this early period of self-enlightenment that I was asked by my state school administrator's association to deliver a series of workshops at a number of locations around the state. The purpose of the workshops was to help building-level school administrators improve their skills as instructional leaders. Now, I must tell you that I feel strongly about the importance of instructional leadership in our schools, but I must also tell you that I have a problem with discussing this topic in public. It seems that I have a predisposition to preach on any topic about which I care deeply—unfortunately, that includes a fairly broad range of topics, because I tend to be a very caring person. At any rate, if I'm not vigilant, suddenly—and without warning—I can find myself preaching rather than teaching.

Apparently, that's exactly what happened to me when I delivered my series of workshops on instructional leadership those many years ago. I was sitting in my office one day after the series had concluded, congratulating myself on the fine job I had done, when I received a piece of correspondence in the mail. The message was simple and straight to the point. The message read, "It's better to know some of the questions than all the answers!" Below this simple message was the inscription "James Thurber (1894–1961)." At first I was thrilled; I thought perhaps James Thurber had sent me the message. But almost instantly, reality set in, and I realized that James couldn't have sent me the message, because he had been dead for quite some time before someone used his sage words to pull me down from my pedestal, plunking me firmly back down on the ground where I belonged. I had been so busy telling everyone the answers to becoming an effective instructional leader that I had forgotten to address the most essential questions.

To this day, I have no idea who sent me that simple but powerful message. At first, I was offended at the implied put-down, but after I'd thought about it for a while, I was grateful. Whoever that thoughtful and caring person was who sent me the message, I want to thank him or her for reminding me that I should be focusing more on the essential questions in my life and not worrying so much about the answers. For although the answers to life's most important questions may vary with the times, the particular circumstances that exist at a given time, or with the persons who are doing the asking or being asked the questions, the essential questions never change. The most essential questions in life never change because they are, by their very nature, eternal.

In her wonderful book, *Leadership and the New Science*, Margaret J. Wheatley (1992) has the following to say about the uncertain nature of life and the futility of wanting someone else to give us the answers to life's most important questions:

> I haven't stopped wanting someone, somewhere to return with the right answers. But I know that my hopes are old, based on a different universe. In this new world, you and I make it up as we go along, not because we lack expertise or planning skills, but because that is the nature of reality.

Reality changes shape and meaning because of our activity. And it is constantly new. We are required to be there, as active participants. It can't happen without us and nobody can do it for us. (p. 151)

I believe (and I don't mean to be preaching here) that the best leaders spend a great deal more time pondering the important questions in life than they do dispensing the correct answers. It's not the right or even the responsibility of a leader to always have the right answers to life's essential questions. It is, however, the responsibility of a leader to acknowledge that these crucial questions exist for every organization and for every individual within an organization. As Collins (2001) notes,

Leading from good to great does not mean coming up with the answers and then motivating everyone to follow your messianic vision. It means having the humility to grasp the fact that you do not yet understand enough to have the answers and then to ask the questions that will lead to the possible insights. (p. 75)

Jack Welch (2005), the highly acclaimed former CEO of General Electric puts it this way:

When you are a leader, your job is to have all the questions. You have to be incredibly comfortable looking like the dumbest person in the room. Every conversation you have about a decision, a proposal, or a piece of market information has to be filled with you saying, "What if?" and "Why not?" and "How come?" (p. 74)

Human experiences in organizations are transitory: it is not the responsibility of the leader to dispense the right answers, but rather, to work faithfully with others in the organization to identify the right questions. Once the right questions have been identified, then everyone working together can seek the answers to those questions that are most relevant to them at a particular time under a prevailing set of circumstances. Ultimately, struggling together with the critical questions will do more to define a successful organization than all the answers in the world. In my view, asking the critical questions in the right ways at the appropriate times helps to define one who is caring enough to lead. Therefore, in the chapters that follow, we will have plenty of opportunities to ponder important questions about caring leadership together. As we embark on our mutual journey, I want to prime you with a single, simple question: So whad'ya know?

TAKE TIME TO REFLECT

1. Chapter 1 asserts that life's essential questions are, by their very nature, eternal. List what you believe are several of life's most essential questions. If you are working with a group, how does your list compare to others' lists? Can (or should) individual circumstances color how we see life's most essential questions?

2. Consider your organization for a moment. What are the essential questions for your organization at this particular moment in time? Are the essential questions different for the major stakeholders in the organization (e.g., the employees, the boss, and the board of directors)?

3. Discuss why it is better to know some of the questions than all of the answers. Give at least one example of a time when you've found this to be true. What were the circumstances that led you to a key realization about the importance of questions?

CHAPTER TWO

WHY AM I GOING TO VISIT BOB?

Several years ago, a wonderful friend and colleague died of Alzheimer's disease. My friend, Bob, and I had worked together for more than fifteen years at the University of South Carolina, and we remained good friends even after his retirement from the university about ten or twelve years ago. For all of you who never had the pleasure of knowing Bob, I can tell you with a high degree of certainty that he was just the kind of guy with whom you'd really enjoy spending time. Bob had that special kind of wisdom about him that comes from living a long, thoughtful, and caring kind of life. He was exceedingly kind, generous to a fault, and had a genuine zest for living. Had Bob been raised in the South, I would have declared him a true Southern gentleman, because he exuded the manners, grace, and style of that rare and dying breed.

One of the things I liked most about Bob was his highly developed sense of humor; he truly loved to laugh. I honestly don't believe that I ever spent more than five or ten minutes with Bob that we didn't laugh together at least once. Whenever I needed a lift, I would seek him out, and he never disappointed. I would always leave his presence feeling a little less anxious about my present circumstances and decidedly more optimistic about my future prospects.

It was shocking to me how quickly the disease ravaged Bob's mind, body, and personality. I had what I thought was a normal conversation with him on the telephone one day in June. But by August of that same year, his beautiful wife of more than fifty years, Barbara, called me in tears to let me know that

6

she had had to place Bob in a care facility because she was no longer able to adequately care for him in their home.

After Bob was institutionalized, I visited him whenever I was near the area where the care facility was located. At first, his physical appearance was about the same as it had always been, and we had nice chats about people, places, and experiences that we had shared over the years. We still laughed together a good bit, although I'm not absolutely certain we were always laughing at the same things at the same time. But that didn't matter all that much at the time. All that mattered was that we enjoyed the visits and had fun together. Sadly, as the weeks and months passed, Bob's physical appearance began to change, the light in his eyes grew dimmer with each subsequent visit, and, little by little, he lost touch with reality until he was no longer able to communicate effectively with the outside world.

The last time I visited with Bob his physical appearance was so altered that I wouldn't have known who he was had I not witnessed the remarkable transformation at short intervals. By this time, the only sounds Bob could make were mostly unintelligible to everyone except Barbara. Bob and Barbara, much like some identical twins, still seemed to share a secret language that allowed them to stay in close touch with each other despite the relentless advancement of the disease. Although I could no longer understand the sounds that came from Bob when he attempted to speak, I still pretended that I knew what he was trying to communicate to me. I gave a little laugh here or inserted a "Yeah, I know" there into the conversation at what I estimated to be the most appropriate points. All the while, Barbara continued to assure me that Bob knew who I was and that he was very glad to see me.

In July of 2000, I moved from South Carolina to Southern California, to accept a new job opportunity. After the move west, I returned periodically to the East Coast for various reasons, and I always made it a point to go by the care facility to spend a little time with Bob and Barbara. Each time, I would telephone Barbara ahead to let her know when I was going to visit Bob so that the three of us could visit together. It meant so much to Barbara that some of Bob's friends and colleagues still spent a little time with him, especially as his illness progressed. I think that Barbara felt that the visits with friends and colleagues restored a little dignity to Bob, by somehow acknowledging that this wonderful human being still existed somewhere inside that spent body confined to a wheelchair.

One of the last times I was scheduled to visit with Bob and Barbara, I had spent the morning with another friend and former colleague of Bob's and was running a little behind schedule. I glanced at my watch and told my friend that I had to get going or I would be late for my visit with Bob. He didn't bother masking the surprised look on his face as he asked, "Why are you going to visit Bob? You know his disease has progressed to the point that he's not even going to know who you are." "I suppose that you're right," I replied in what probably sounded like an apologetic tone. But then I added quickly, "He probably won't know who I am, but Barbara will, and it's important to her that people still care enough about Bob to come and spend some time with him. I guess that at this point, I'm visiting Bob more for Barbara's sake than I am for Bob's." My friend nodded his acceptance of this line of reasoning and I hurried to my car.

When I arrived for my visit, Bob, Barbara, and I sat together in the large family room of the care facility with about fifteen other Alzheimer's patients. Out of the corner of my eye, I noticed a tiny, silver-haired woman sitting in a wheelchair, watching us closely from the far side of the room. As Barbara and I talked about items of common interest and Bob occasionally added his own unique input to the conversation, I noticed that this elderly woman in a wheelchair was slowly moving closer and closer to where the three of us were sitting. She shuffled her feet along the floor almost imperceptibly, and, inch by inch, she drew closer.

After a time, this silver-haired woman was positioned directly behind me in her wheelchair. Then suddenly, and without warning, she slid her arm through an opening in the back of the chair in which I was sitting, placed her hand squarely on top of my hand, and leaned her head against the back of my right shoulder! I didn't know exactly what I should say or do, but it was very clear to me that this woman was desperately in need of a little human contact. So I placed a hand on top of hers, and we remained locked together in that unusual embrace for the rest of my visit with Bob and Barbara.

After the visit, when I was walking across the parking lot of the care facility to my car, I thought about Bob's illness, my periodic visits over the past couple of years, and what it all had meant. At that moment, I came to the conclusion that I wasn't visiting Bob just for Bob's sake—most likely, he didn't know, and he probably didn't even care who I was at that point in his life. I also realized that I wasn't visiting Bob just for Barbara's sake. Although I sensed that my visits were extremely important to her, and I genuinely wanted to help ease her burden, I wasn't visiting her husband just to satisfy her needs. No! That definitely wasn't it! I wasn't there primarily for Bob or for Barbara. The honest truth is that I was there for me! I was there because I want to be the kind of person who continues to care about his friends and colleagues even after they are no longer capable of returning that caring in the same way. I want to be the kind of person who has the capacity to give without expecting anything in return. I want to be the kind of person who is sensitive to the needs of others and caring enough to want to meet those needs in the best way that I can.

You see, my being there was tangible evidence for me that I am becoming more like the person that I ultimately want to be. Although anyone who knows me well will tell you that I have a long way to go on the journey to becoming the person I want to be, it was somehow comforting for me at that precise moment to know that I was at least moving in the right direction. I would wager most of us don't get these kinds of confirmations nearly as often as we would like in our everyday lives, so when we do they are very special moments indeed. These moments act as signposts to let us know that we are on our chosen paths toward becoming the human beings that we want to become.

Now that Bob has passed away and I am looking back on these experiences, I realize more than ever that Bob and Barbara were not the primary beneficiaries of my visits. I was the primary beneficiary! After more than sixty years of experiencing much of what life has to offer, I have come to believe that the only real joy in life comes from living a life that matters. People live lives that matter by doing meaningful things for others. Visiting Bob gave me a golden opportunity to demonstrate to myself that I genuinely cared enough to do something meaningful for my friend. Consequently, visiting Bob gave me great joy. In the end, I came to realize that this was Bob's gift to me

By this time, you are no doubt wondering, "What in the world does all this have to do with leadership?" My reply is simple: "Going to visit Bob has everything to do with leadership!" It has everything to do with leadership because every one of us is on the way to visit Bob. Regardless of who we are, each of us is inexorably moving along on our individual life's journey toward becoming the friend, student, parent, lover, colleague, spouse, leader, and, ultimately, the human being that we want to be. Nobody can choose the best paths for us to follow on this journey: we have to choose our own paths.

Occasionally, there will be times on our journey when we race ahead, sure that we are going in the right direction. There will also be times when we stumble and fall, and still other times when we become so totally disoriented that we temporarily lose our way. All the while, however, we must remember that it's all about the journey, not the destination. We have to be patient and look out for the signposts (such as the one that Bob gave to me) along the way to reassure us that we are, after all, moving in the right direction.

In the future, should someone ask me, "Why are you going to visit Bob?" surely I will have a much better answer. How about you? Below, and in the chapters to follow, I will suggest some signposts for you in the form of critical questions and brief exercises. I sincerely hope that you will take the time to consider the questions and complete the exercises. Perhaps in this way you will be able to create a personal journal to help document precisely where you are on the path that you have chosen on your journey to becoming the leader and the person that you ultimately want to become.

TAKE TIME TO REFLECT

1. Describe in a few brief paragraphs the kind of person and leader that you ultimately want to become. How far do you feel you have moved along the path to reach your desired destination? Has your personal path taken you on some unexpected detours as you have continued to grow and develop? What were some of these detours, and what special insights did you gain from these experiences in terms of who you are becoming as a leader and a person?

2. In a way, Bob was a moral compass for the author in that he provided a positive signpost to let him know that he was moving along the right path to becoming the kind of friend that he wanted to become. Of course, we sometimes also see negative signposts that tell us that we may be headed in the wrong direction. Choose a role that you are presently playing in life—parent, teacher, leader, friend, spouse, and so on—and list one or two signposts on both sides (positive and negative) that have helped you get a fix on where you are on your journey to becoming the person you want to be in whatever role you have chosen. If you are working with a group, share your story with others if you are comfortable doing so.

CHAPTER THREE

WHAT IS A LEADER?

Like most human beings that I have known, I have been blessed many, many times in my life. One of my most cherished blessings is that I was fortunate enough to be born in a community situated directly beside the Atlantic Ocean. As I write this chapter, it's early March, and I'm back in my hometown for a few days, ensconced in a seaside beach home belonging to a couple of my oldest and dearest friends. After nearly a week of rain and cold weather, this morning broke as a bright and beautiful spring day. From time to time, I can't resist putting down my pen and looking out the window toward the ocean. A steady Northeaster is blowing across the magnificent landscape. Each time I look up from my work, the sea oats are waving to me, beckoning me to come out and play. The golden sun is streaming down on the blue-green surf, which is pounding out a steady rhythm against the gleaming white sand, while squadrons of pelicans fly by in their V-shaped formations as if on some secret search-and-destroy mission. It takes all the self-control I can muster to resist the sea oats and the sand, the surf and the pelicans. But I need to be strong this morning. I must direct all my energy toward exploring a difficult question, the answer to which has eluded countless others far more enlightened than me for centuries. The question I am referring to is, "What is a leader?"

More than forty years ago, I was happy to be back in this small seaside city where I spent my youth. I had returned to my hometown on leave from active duty in the United States Navy. It was the early 1960s. The Vietnam War was heating up, and the air squadron in which I served had just returned to the United States after a year-long cruise aboard an aircraft carrier in the

South China Sea. When you're nineteen or twenty years old, a year out of your life is a long time indeed. I felt as if I had been away forever. I couldn't wait to get back to my roots. I was desperate to touch base with some of my old high school buddies and to get back down on the beach, where I could feel I was home again, at long last.

As soon as I arrived at my parents' home, I got on the phone and started calling all my old friends around town, hoping to catch up on everything I had missed during the eternity that I had been away. As luck would have it, one of my best friends was just leaving his house with his fiancée to go for a ride on the beach in his jeep. He invited me to ride along.

A Northeaster had been pummeling the coast for several days. The powerful wind and the wild surf made for an exciting and highly entertaining afternoon for the three of us in the jeep. We saw all kinds of interesting things as we rode up and down and over and around the sand dunes. There were fat, green, slimy mounds of seaweed; a virtual fortune in sand dollars; lots of pointy, brown starfish; a variety of colorful and unusual seashells; and even a dead porpoise that had washed up among the collage of sea artifacts displayed along the shore. As we rounded the jetties that protected the inlet into the harbor at the north end of the beach, we were surprised to see an abandoned shrimp boat that had grounded itself on the rocks of the jetty about one hundred yards offshore. The punishing winds and driving currents had succeeded in dismantling a portion of the outer shell of the boat, and some of the planks had already washed up on the beach by the time we arrived on the scene. We paused in our journey for some time to speculate about what may have caused the boat to founder, and we wondered out loud about the fate of the crew members that had been on board.

It was at this juncture that we saw something we had never seen before in all our many years of exploring the beach: a huge dead octopus blown ashore by the strong winds. The octopus formed a large, gray lump on the smooth white surface of the beach, even though it was partially buried by the wet sand. The sight was so unusual that it compelled the three of us to get out of the jeep and conduct a closer inspection. We poked and prodded the dead creature with sticks and stretched it out until it extended over a diameter of six or eight feet. We were all pretty excited by the find, but my friend's fiancée was beside herself with amazement. When she saw the strange animal fully extended, she exclaimed, "My God—would you look at those huge testicles!" While struggling to suppress his laughter, my friend quickly corrected his betrothed, "Tentacles, honey! Tentacles!" he said.

The young woman had made a humorous but common mistake, a mistake that is unremarkable to all of us as we constantly seek to understand and explain to others the range of mysterious and wonderful things that we encounter in our everyday lives. Frequently, when we encounter something with which we are unfamiliar or that we don't fully understand, we may not even know what we're looking at! And even if we do know what we're looking at, we may not know what to call it! In many ways, leadership is an octopus. It's much easier to recognize it when we see it than it is to understand it or to explain it to others.

That being said, let us briefly explore together some of the characteristics and qualities of leadership from the perspectives of some of those who have studied it, written about it, experienced it, or practiced it. Together, we will poke it and prod it a bit. If we're extremely lucky, maybe we'll even be able to spread out its tentacles until we can make out a faint outline on the sand of this thing called leadership.

Of course, most of us are familiar with the routine dictionary-type definitions of leadership that talk about leaders as special people who somehow get things done through others, or as those who have the skills to move a group of people toward a common goal, to take people in a direction that they may not otherwise choose to go. Based on a review of a series of leadership studies, Hogan, Curphy, and Hogan (1994) suggest, for example, that "leadership involves persuading other people to set aside for a period of time their individual concerns and to pursue a common goal that is important for the responsibilities and welfare of a group" (p. 493). The key to a leader's effectiveness, according to these writers, is "his or her ability to build a team" (p. 499) in order to get things done.

Although most of us would agree that leaders are able to get things done in one way or another, such definitions don't shed much light on the essential nature of leadership. Perhaps we can gain a little more perspective if we think about the evolution of the concepts of leaders and leadership over time. The discussion of leaders and leadership is thousands of years old. Men, women, and even children have been leading for as long as human beings have banded together and worked cooperatively, initially in an effort to survive and later also to improve the quality of life. Countless studies have tried to determine what causes or allows some people to lead and others to follow. Although much has been learned about leaders and leading, for the most part, leadership remains an intriguing mystery.

Throughout the last century, the literature has chronicled some interesting twists and turns in the study of leadership and the posing of leadership theories. Beginning with the great man theory (as far as I can determine, there was no great woman theory), which postulates that leaders are born and not made, the study of leadership has progressed through a series of distinct phases as the thinking about leaders and leadership has become more sophisticated, if not more valid.

The trait theory, the successor to the great man theory, suggests that the behaviors of successful leaders can be attributed to a set of unique personality traits such as forcefulness, intelligence, and the need for achievement. The development of measurement indices in the field of psychology coincided with the birth of the trait theory and provided the impetus for the idea of studying leaders by measuring the presence or absence of certain traits using tools such as checklists, tests, rating scales, and interviews.

The work of Frederick Taylor and others during the early twentieth century gave rise to a school of thinkers in the field of leadership studies that came to be known as the behavioral theorists. The behavioral theorists include a distinguished list of notables: Argyris, Blake, Mouton, Getzels, Guba, Likert, and McGregor. These researchers believed that what leaders do is far more significant than any set of traits they might possess. Consequently, they focused their research on the development of leadership styles and leader behavior. The behaviorists recognized that although organizations might be rigid, human beings within those organizations have needs that must be addressed if the organizations are to be successful and productive. From the work of the behavioral theorists came a series of leadership models, assessment tools, and motivational theories that have had enormous influence on the study and practice of leadership to the present day.

Situational or contingency leadership theory evolved during the 1960s from the work of the behavioral theorists and questioned whether there is one best way for a leader to lead in all situations. Situational theorists such as Fiedler, Hersey, and Blanchard maintained that effective leadership behavior is dependent on the situation in which the leader operates and must take into account variables such as the nature of the tasks to be performed, the maturity of the group, and operative time constraints. Situational leadership theory emphasizes the need for leaders to alter approaches to leadership based on the circumstances in a particular situation in order to realize optimal results.

Some of the descriptions of leaders and leadership postulated during the past decade or two are not only quite different, they are intriguing in that they focus more on who leaders are rather than what they are able to do through others. For example, Sergiovanni (1992) says that "the heart of leadership has to do with what a person believes, values, dreams about, and is committed to—the person's personal vision, to use the popular term" (p. 7).

Sergiovanni (1992) describes leaders as the first followers in the sense that "followership requires an emotional commitment to a set of ideas" (p. 71). As he points out, "Hierarchical position and personality are not enough to earn one the mantle of leader. Instead, it comes through one's demonstrated devotion and success as a follower. The true leader is the one who follows first" (p. 72). By linking the importance of beliefs, values, and dreams to leadership behaviors, Sergiovanni stresses the importance of joining the heart and the head of leadership with the hand of leadership. In this way, leaders become authetic to those who are inspired to follow them, because the things that leaders do reflect what both the leaders and the followers think, feel, and believe. In this way, a leader's actions, decisions, and behaviors can more easily be understood, respected, and appreciated by those who follow. This results in a covenantal community whose nature, Sergiovanni suggests, is in some ways more sacred than it is secular.

Max De Pree (1989), the noted management expert and former CEO of Herman Miller, one of the most successful corporate entities in the world under his leadership, has expressed the belief that leadership is not a science: "Leadership is much more an art, a belief, a condition of the heart, than a set of things to do" (p. 148). To De Pree, leaders are servants to their followers in that they seek to remove the obstacles that prevent them from doing their jobs and to give them the freedom and incentive to live up to their potential while they complete themselves as human beings. In De Pree's words, "The first responsibility of a leader is to define reality. The last is to say thank you. In between the two, the leader must become a servant and a debtor" (p. 11). He further asserts, "Leaders owe the organization a new reference point for what caring, purposeful, committed people can be in an institutional setting" (p. 15). Leaders must help to define a set of clear organizational values, encourage contrary opinions, provide joy, respect all individuals, communicate effectively, and, in every way possible, take full advantage of the opportunities that leadership provides to "make a meaningful difference in the lives of those who permit leaders to lead" (p. 22). Like Sergiovanni (1992), De Pree believes that effective leadership ultimately depends on a covenantal relationship between leaders and followers based on a common core of shared values. A common core of shared values implies that there is a high level of communication between leaders and followers that results in a clear understanding and acceptance of those shared values.

Collins (2001) in his very revealing book, *Good to Great*, describes in detail how some corporations are able to make great leaps in performance, thereby becoming highly successful in comparison to their competitors while maintaining their dominant positions in the marketplace over extended periods. While Collins and his research team initially sought to "downplay the role of top executives so that we could avoid the simplistic 'credit the leader' or 'blame the leader' thinking common today" (p. 21), they found that the data were so strong regarding the impact of leadership on fostering the transition of companies from good to great that a closer examination of leaders and leadership was required.

Based on their research, Collins and his colleagues came up with a five-level pyramid of leadership types in a hierarchical arrangement. From the lowest to the highest level, the leaders at the various stages of leadership were termed Highly Capable Individual, Contributing Team Member, Competent Manager, Effective Leader, and Level 5 Executive. Level 5 leaders, as defined by Collins (2001), had qualities in common that set them apart from other successful leaders that we generally think of as effective, and great companies as identified in Collins's research all had Level 5 leaders while the comparison companies in the study did not.

> The good-to-great executives were all cut from the same cloth. It didn't matter whether the company was consumer or industrial, in crisis or steady state, offered services or products. It didn't matter when the transition took place or how big the company. All the good-to-great companies had Level 5 leadership at the time of transition. Furthermore, the absence of Level 5 leadership showed up as a consistent pattern in the comparison companies. (p. 22)

While Level 5 leaders embody all the positive qualities of the leaders from the other four levels, they also have a unique combination of two special qualities that set them apart. Those qualities are expressed eloquently by Collins (2001) by the simple formula **"HUMILITY + WILL = LEVEL 5"** (p. 22). The good-to-great Level 5 leaders were marked not by personal ambition, but by what Collins terms professional will.

While most of us would expect that our leaders would be willful, the idea of willful and humble in combination is more than a little counterintuitive. But on closer examination, pairing willful and humble makes perfect sense if we think of willful as being determined and persistent in pursuit of universally held organizational goals and values. Willful in this sense is not about the leader succeeding—it is about the organization succeeding through achieving its purpose and accomplishing its mission. This concept of willful stands in stark contrast to the concept of willful as it is embodied in a leader who is aggressive and competitive, a leader wanting to win at all costs in order to gratify his or her ego rather than to advance the goals and values of the organization.

Collins (2001) effectively makes the point that the very best leaders are not the "larger-than-life saviors" with "big personalities," rather they are "a study in duality: modest and willful, humble and fearless" (p. 22). In my view, caring is central to Level 5 leadership because the things that one cares about, how much one cares, and how that caring is ultimately expressed determines the capacity not just to lead fearlessly, but to lead with humility and a deep sense of caring. I am also convinced that caring determines the extent to which others willingly follow a leader. I will have a good deal more to say about this in subsequent chapters, but first, let's take a look at how caring is reflected in the leadership views of several outstanding educational leaders.

Walt Tobin, who was selected State Superintendent of the Year on several occasions by various organizations and has served as president of the super-intendent's association in South Carolina, has described leadership in terms of what he calls soft skills. If you ask his opinion about what makes some leaders better than others, he will likely rattle off a laundry list of attributes such as integrity, trust, dependability, fairness, honesty, dignity, and visibility. These attributes have little to do with what a leader knows or even does, but a lot to do with the kind of human being the leader is. Tobin says that leaders must find out what's important to others and then make it important to themselves. He suggests that aside from all the tools required for successful leadership, successful leaders are able to find joy in what they're doing. As he put it, "After more than thirty years, I still love to hear a first grader read."

Michele Forman, 2001 National Teacher of the Year and an outstanding teacher leader, when asked, defined teacher leadership as follows:

Teacher leadership means first of all staying focused on students and their learning. Student learning is the reason schools exist and teachers teach. A teacher leader models excellence in teaching and under-stands the extraordinary potential of each learner, the tentative nature of knowledge, and the necessity of continuous growth and renewal as a professional. . . . True leaders reject hierarchy and value others' abilities and contributions. They celebrate the creativity and the challenge of good teaching and exhibit enormous reserves of intellectual, emotional, and physical energy that fuel their own growth, even as they nurture their students and support their colleagues. . . . Teacher leaders appreci-ate the importance and dignity of their work. They know they make a difference. (Personal communication, October 25, 2002)

When asked to give her views on the essential elements of effective lead-ership, Cynthia Cervantes McGuire, Superintendent of the Azusa Unified School District in California, described leadership as "giving to others; it's realizing who you are and keeping in touch with your inner core; it's making mistakes, failing, and succeeding. . . . Leadership is also following; it's hav-ing spirit and soul. It's giving back tenfold what was given you." Cervantes McGuire regards leadership as "a journey through uncharted waters requiring guts and courage." Most important, however, she feels that leadership is "about staying in love with what you do." You can feel Cervantes McGuire's love for serving others in several comments she made as she accepted an award as Manager of the Year in her school district back when she was serving as an elementary school principal:

> There are times, as I'm rising early in the morning, that I lament the fact that I've not yet won the lottery. And then as I get closer to my exit on the 210 freeway, I take great comfort in the recognition that I do have riches untold. I work with people—colleagues and community—that I consider friends and family. I work with people of uncommon spirit and unending purpose. I am rich! (Personal communication, March 6, 1999)

The love that Cervantes McGuire feels for her work is also generously reflected in the voices of those she works with on a daily basis. After all, who is better qualified to judge a person's leadership than the beneficiaries of that leadership? Below are excerpts from several letters that were written by some of those who were touched by Cervantes McGuire's outstanding leadership—a parent, a teacher, and a staff member—supporting her nomination as Manager of the Year:

> Thank you Mrs. Cervantes McGuire for being the kind of person that a parent would choose to care for her children. . . . You make time to spend with students and really listen to them. . . . You have set goals and standards, implemented programs, and coalesced the staff into a truly remarkable teaching team sharing the common goal of always striving to provide the best for children. I am so pleased and honored to have the privilege of knowing you, and to have you in my children's lives. (School site council member and parent)

> I have been touched by the many gifts Cynthia brings to school and shares in her work. Cynthia has a gift for making each staff member feel valued and vital to our school community. Cynthia's thoughts, concerns, and actions always represent the deep commitment which she has to the lives of students as well as staff. Cynthia navigates the roles of manager and friend very well. At times I am not sure who is supporting me, Cynthia the manager or Cynthia the friend. It is this personal quality of her leadership that I admire and value most. She is a beacon of encouragement with whom I am honored and blessed to work so closely. (First-year teacher)

> A good leader is one who has an open mind, a compassionate heart, and a willingness to listen. Cynthia has all those qualities and much more!

When asking opinions or thoughts from employees, students, and parents, her consideration is sincere—never undermining of one's position. Cynthia has the ability to make us all feel important and valued as instructional aides and parents, but more important, as people. (Parent and instructional aide)

In all these statements of support, one sees a common thread of love and genuine caring reflected back from the recipients of Cervantes McGuire's leadership, regardless of their roles in the school community. One sees a confirmation of Sergiovanni's (1992) and De Pree's (1989) concept of moral leadership in an organization that is nurtured and sustained by a common set of beliefs, values, and dreams that have helped to create an organization that is more like a family than it is like a public institution.

A few years ago, a friend and colleague took a trip to visit her daughter in Atlanta. The daughter had recently purchased a home and invited her mother to come and see her place. It was arranged that the daughter would meet her mother on the edge of town and lead her to the daughter's new home. The two met at the appointed time and place as planned, and the daughter took the lead and pulled out into heavy rush-hour traffic on the expressway. My friend described for me how her daughter drove in and out of the traffic at increasingly higher rates of speed. At first, her daughter was going fifty miles per hour, then sixty, seventy, and finally eighty! My friend became more and more concerned as she vainly tried to keep pace with her speeding daughter.

Suddenly, my friend came to the realization that she was being foolhardy by trying to follow behind her daughter in heavy traffic at such excessive speeds. As she later put it, "My daughter is twenty-five years old—she's entitled to act foolishly. But I'm fifty! I asked myself, what kind of fool would be risking her life chasing after someone in rush-hour traffic on an expressway in Atlanta?" As soon as my friend came to this realization, she pulled off the expressway at the next exit, went to a nearby shopping mall, and spent the next several hours shopping. When she felt that her daughter had had sufficient time to agonize over her missing mother, my friend called her from her cell phone and informed the young woman of her whereabouts. When the relieved daughter arrived at the mall to retrieve her mother, my friend had some carefully chosen words for her:

I was in a vulnerable situation not being acquainted with how to get to your house in the unfamiliar, rush-hour traffic. I trusted you to lead me, but you didn't care enough to maintain close contact with me. You went on your own merry way without even so much as a backward glance in the mirror to see if I were following or if I needed your help. When I became convinced that you weren't concerned about me, that you apparently didn't care about my needs, I made a decision to stop following you. Do you think that you are now able to lead me to your home in a responsible and caring way? (Personal communication, March 1998)

Needless to say, after this little object lesson, the daughter was a caring and considerate leader as she guided her mother from the mall parking lot to her home. She checked her rearview mirror frequently and adjusted her speed to make sure that she never again lost contact with her mother. In due time, both leader and follower arrived safely at their destination.

There is a valuable lesson in this little story for all those who desire to lead. Leadership requires a high level of care and concern on the part of the leader for those who would choose to follow. Whenever a leader fails to exercise the level of care and concern required to maintain close contact with his or her followers, the implied contract between the leader and followers is voided. Contrary to popular opinion, true leaders are never far out in front of others, as we so often hear people say that they are. Rather, the best leaders are precisely in the middle of the beliefs, dreams, and values of those whom they lead. Beliefs, dreams, and values don't belong just to the leader or to the followers. They must, in fact, be shared!

Permission to lead can come only through the consent of those who willingly give up their right to go off in their own directions in favor of going in the group's direction. As they move forward, leaders must constantly look to their left and to their right and occasionally behind them to make sure that they are still at the center of the group. The moment they lose contact with the beliefs and goals and dreams of those who make up the group, the implied contract between leader and follower is no longer valid and leaders thereby lose their capacity to lead.

A couple of years ago, I had the good fortune to be seated next to James MacGregor Burns at a luncheon. Burns has been regarded as perhaps the foremost presidential scholar who ever lived, and his book, so simply titled *Leadership* (1978), won both the Pulitzer Prize and a National Book Award. Naturally, I took advantage of the fortuitous circumstance provided by our close proximity to question Burns about some of his ideas on leadership. I had read his book, and I knew how he had defined leadership in his writing. I knew, for example, that he regarded power and leadership as separate entities: "Power wielders may treat people as things. Leaders may not. All leaders are actual or potential power holders, but not all power holders are leaders" (p. 18). I also knew that Burns's view of leadership had a decidedly ethical core:

The crucial variable again is purpose. . . . I define leadership as leaders inducing followers to act for certain goals that represent the values and the motivations—the wants and needs, the aspirations and expectations—of both leaders and followers. And the genius of leadership lies in the manner in which leaders see and act on their own and their followers' values and motivations. (p. 19)

So when I asked Burns that day to define leadership for me and to tell me how one would go about recognizing a leader, his straightforward answer didn't really surprise me. He thought for a moment, and then he said, "Leadership is first and foremost a moral act. Above all, leaders must be virtuous." Although it had been about twenty-five years since Burns had written his landmark book on leadership, his ideas about leadership remained essentially unchanged. In a fundamental sense, Burns blazed the trail for all those who have come along in the past several decades by defining leadership in terms such as *moral, servant, transformational*, and even *soulful*.

Clearly, the literature reveals many differing perspectives on leaders and leadership. While there are many commonalities used by writers and thinkers (these are not necessarily the same individuals, by the way) to describe leaders and leadership, there are just as many differences. Welch (2005) has thusly summed up the leadership equation:

And yet, good leadership happens—and it comes in all kinds of packages. There are quiet leaders and bombastic ones. There are analytical leaders and more impulsive ones. Some are tough as nails with their teams, others more nurturing. On the surface, you would be hard-pressed to say what qualities these leaders share. Underneath, you would surely see the best care passionately about their people—about their growth and success. (p. 79)

My study of leaders and leadership over the past thirty-five years leads me to endorse the concepts of leadership as described by writers and thinkers such as Burns (1978), Sergiovanni (1992), Collins (2001), De Pree (1989), and Welch (2005). Leadership is so much more than a title or a formal mandate to take charge in a particular situation. It is more than a discrete set of personal qualities or traits or the ability to perform a set of complex tasks. Leadership at its best involves more than the will of a single person to direct a group in a specific direction. I believe that the true essence of leadership is a directed "group will" bound together by common needs, goals, beliefs, and values. To me, leadership is the ability to help create a shared vision. It is the ability to see and to help others see beyond the present realities, and to help them glimpse the unlimited possibilities in the future.

The one thing I am fairly certain about at this point is that leadership is much more than someone in a leadership role saying, knowing, or doing things. Of course all leaders say, know, and do things in the name of leadership. But at its core, leadership requires a great deal more than saying, knowing, or doing—leadership is about being. I believe that Cashman (1998) has it right when he says, "Leadership is not simply something we do. It comes from somewhere inside us. Leadership is a process, an intimate expression of who we are. It is our being in action" (p. 18). Cashman has also expressed the view that the essential difference between a leader and a manager is not so much in what gets done in an organization, but in how it gets done. "Managers control by virtue of their doing. Leaders control by virtue of their being" (p. 47).

In the simplest terms, a leader is someone people want to follow rather than someone they have to follow. Furthermore, I am convinced that the best leaders make others around them in an organization want to be better, both in terms of what they do and in terms of who they are as human beings. I believe that this ability to inspire people to want to be better and to perform better is perhaps the greatest attribute any leader can possess. It is the ultimate compliment to a leader when she or he is able to inspire others in the organization to want to be better, because individuals striving together to become better is the X factor that sets organizations apart, ultimately dividing them into winners and losers.

What do you believe are the essential characteristics of effective leadership? Do you know leadership when you see it? If so, do you know what to call it? Do you have a pretty good idea about the values, beliefs, and dreams of those who work with you in your organization? Do you make it a point to share your own values, beliefs, and dreams with your colleagues on a regular basis? Do you have a genuine appreciation for the great debt that leaders owe to those who trust them enough to allow them to lead? Do you derive a sense of satisfaction and even a measure of joy from the privilege of serving others in a leadership role? Do you accept the responsibility to help people become the very best that they can be? Are you constantly looking to your right and to your left and occasionally checking your rearview mirror to be sure that you are still in the middle of the values, beliefs, and dreams of those who have trusted you to lead? The carefully chosen questions in the ensuing chapters will provide you with ample opportunities to test yourself against these demanding standards.

TAKE TIME TO REFLECT

1. Take a few moments to think about some of the most outstanding leaders you have been exposed to during your life. Whom do you regard as one of the most outstanding leaders with whom you have ever been privileged to work? What set this leader apart? What were the unique qualities or characteristics that defined her or him as a leader and made this leader so special?

2. Sometimes we learn as much and perhaps even more from bad role models as we learn from good role models. Describe a leader with whom you've worked in the past who you regard as being ineffective. In your opinion, what were the qualities and characteristics, or lack thereof, that made this person an ineffective leader?

CHAPTER FOUR

WHY SHOULD LEADERS CARE ABOUT CARING?

Most people have a favorite relative who is special to them in one way or another. I know that I do. My favorite relative was an uncle on my mother's side of the family. My uncle, Cecil Yelvington, was special to me because he let me know that he cared about me, and that I was special to him. I knew that I was special to him because, from the time that I was a small child, he did little things to let me know that he cared, like pulling a shiny quarter "out of my ear" and giving it to me, or saving me the prize from his cereal box, or bringing me a Hershey's chocolate bar whenever he came to visit our family. Uncle Cecil sometimes let me ride in the basket on the front of his bicycle when we went to the barbershop for a haircut. He took me fishing and taught me how to shoot a shotgun. When I think back to those times, I realize that Cecil Yelvington was more than just my favorite uncle: in many ways, he was like a father to me.

Like many of his generation, Uncle Cecil was not a well-educated man in a formal sense. In fact, he never even finished elementary school. But my uncle was a smart man, and he was curious enough to want to learn about the world around him. Because of his curiosity, he gained a great deal of knowledge about a lot of things. One could legitimately describe him as being well self-educated. In many ways, Cecil Yelvington was about as self-sufficient as anyone I have ever known. He could do almost anything that needed to be done: fix a car, build a house, or grow a vegetable garden. He had an extraordinarily keen sense of humor, and his quick wit could make anybody laugh.

Cecil Yelvington was also a very proud man. There were two things in his life of which he was most proud. One was his World War II service as a soldier in Patton's Third Army. I often regret that I didn't ask my uncle more about the war and his role as an infantryman in Africa and Italy. The second great source of pride for this special man was his vocation. Uncle Cecil worked most of his life as a carpenter for the Florida East Coast Railway. Whenever someone would ask my uncle what he did for a living, he would proudly proclaim, "I'm a carpenter by trade." He was never just a "carpenter"; he was always a "carpenter by trade." He took great pride in his trade and felt that every project he undertook was a testament to his worth, both as a man and as a craftsman.

I used to watch my uncle hang doors, and I marveled at the care he took to do the job as well as it could possibly be done. Whenever Cecil hung a door, he would measure the opening for the door and then mark and cut the door slightly larger than the opening. Next, he would place the door against the opening and measure it once again. Then he would take the door down and plane the door edges until he felt it was a little closer to being a fit. He would then place the door against the opening again, take it down, plane a little more, place it against the opening again, take it down, plane a little more, and repeat the process as many times as it took to get a perfect fit between the door and the opening. When it fit perfectly, Cecil would chisel out little recessed areas for the hinges so that they would fit flush against the wood. Finally, he would sand all the rough spots out of the wood and hang the door from its hinges. When Cecil Yelvington was done hanging a door, not only did it fit the door opening perfectly, but it was so well balanced that a person could gently push the door with an index finger and it would smoothly swing shut with a crisp snap of the latch. When closed, the door would be equidistant from the door casing all the way around the outside edges, and it would be snug, but not too snug, when resting against the doorjamb.

Have you recently looked at how the doors are hung in your home or in your workplace? Do most of these doors look as if they had been hung by someone who genuinely cared—by a carpenter by trade? I shopped for a home in Southern California several years ago and I was astounded, not just by the outrageous prices, but also by the poor quality of the workmanship I observed as my wife and I traveled with our realtor from house to house. Rarely did I see a door that would do justice to my Uncle Cecil. Many doors had cracks of half an inch or more between the door and the door casing at one end of the top of the door while they dragged against the door casing at the other extreme. It was a certainty that no mortal human was ever going to close some of these doors with a single index finger!

So why tell this story to you? What difference does taking great care to hang a door properly have to do with leadership? I'm telling you this story for three reasons: First, I want to provide an illustration of a man who was highly engaged with his work, a man who loved his work and who took great pride in doing his work the best it could possibly be done because he felt that, when the job was complete, the quality of the work was a direct reflection on him. Consequently, he did his work very well because he cared deeply what his boss as well as others thought about the quality of his work, and, indirectly, he also cared what they thought about him as a carpenter and as a man. More important, he cared what he thought about himself. After all, Cecil Yelvington wasn't merely a carpenter—he was a carpenter by trade.

The second point I want to make is that many, if not most, people are not actively engaged in the work that they do each day. Csikszentmihalyi (2003) says that "most work is either so dull and uninspiring that doing one's best still means using less than 10 percent of one's potentiality, or is so stressful that it sucks the worker's life energy dry" (p. 30). Csikszentmihalyi goes on to say,

> So one of the intriguing paradoxes of the human condition is that while surveys indicate that about 80 percent of adults claim that they would continue to work even if they had so much money that they didn't have to worry about having more, the majority can hardly wait each day to leave their job and go home. (p. 86)

What's wrong with this picture? The great majority of people say they want to work, but they hate their jobs!

This leads me to the third point I want to make: Leaders are responsible for establishing the conditions in the workplace that cause organizations to be great places to work, thereby making it more likely that employees will be highly engaged with their work and will perform to the best of their ability.

When leaders fail to make work rewarding and even enjoyable for employees, Csikszentmihalyi (2003) suggests, employees will try to get by with as little effort as possible: "Cutting corners, passing the buck, malingering, and taking advantage of the job are often considered canny moves—a way to beat the system" (p. 104). But work doesn't have to be that way. Leaders can develop workplaces where employees enjoy their work, take great pride in doing it well, and experience personal growth and satisfaction in the process. I am convinced that the simple act of caring is a leader's single most powerful tool for creating a workplace environment in which employees feel appreciated and respected, resulting in a workforce that is highly engaged and productive.

The preponderance of available evidence clearly illustrates that when workers are highly engaged with their work, they are happier and more productive and the organizations that employ them are, in turn, more productive and more successful. The key determinant of a great place to work is the level of employee engagement.

Employee engagement is defined by Howe (2003) as

the state of emotional and intellectual involvement that workers have in an organization. Engaged employees are those individuals who want to and do take action to improve the business results of their organization. Three key behaviors demonstrate employee engagement in an organization:

1. *Say.* Employees speak positively about the organization to coworkers, potential employees and customers.

2. *Stay.* Employees have an intense desire to be part of the organization.

3. *Strive.* Employees exert extra effort and take on work that contributes to employer success. (p. 41)

The above, quoted in Howe's article, is from the preliminary findings of the fifth annual Best Employers in Canada study (Best Employers in Canada, 2007), sponsored by Hewitt Associates Canada; the report was written to the International Foundation. In the study, four years of Canadian and globally collected data were analyzed to determine what factors made organizations great places to work. As noted, the key ingredient of a great place to work was the level of employee engagement that resulted in employees who spoke positively about their organizations, wanted to remain a part of the organization, and worked hard to contribute to the success of the organization. What leader or what organization wouldn't want highly engaged workers? More important, what determines whether or not employees will be highly engaged with their work?

According to the preliminary findings of this study, there is no universal recipe for becoming a best employer. Rather, each organization must develop its own unique solution to creating a work environment that leads to highly engaged employees. However, senior leadership of the best employers, as identified in the study, did believe that employee engagement was essential for business success. Leadership was, therefore, motivated to invest in the practices necessary to bring about engagement. As reported in the study and as discussed by Howe (2003, p. 42), a summary of practices leading to a high level of employee engagement included

1. Having a process to perpetuate the people-related values they hold dearly and holding leaders responsible for extending and enforcing behaviors that reinforce those values throughout the organization

2. Skill at executing the core people practices such as the day-to-day application of recognition, performance management, employee development, sharing the direction of the company, and aligning people to the business goals

3. Investing the time, effort, and resources required to make the success of the business a personal issue for their employees by enabling them to take responsibility for their contributions to the goals of the organization through the provision of proper authority, resources, and decision-making power

4. Having and communicating a clear understanding of their business model through a clear vision of what they are trying to achieve in every aspect of the business, while aligning the component pieces and executing the details

When asked to describe the most significant people issues they faced, leaders participating in the study responded with the following five most frequently cited issues, in order, they were

1. Attracting the right people with the right skills

2. Retaining employees

3. Developing people's skills and capabilities

4. Successfully managing change

5. Motivating/engaging employees to support the organization's business direction. (Howe, 2003, p. 42)

The findings of the study indicated that the best employers were in a better position to deal with these issues than were their competitors. Beyond these obvious advantages, however, the study's authors suggested that "if employers are looking for a more concrete reason to work toward being a best employer, the fact that these companies have better financial returns is a persuasive argument. . . . The bottom line is that being a best employer carries decided benefits for organizations, employees, shareholders and customers" (Howe, 2003, p. 43).

Clearly, engagement of employees is critical for organizations because effort is directly linked to engagement. As Kahn (1990) notes,

> People can use varying degrees of their selves, physically, cognitively, and emotionally, in the roles they perform, even as they maintain the integrity of the boundaries between who they are and the roles they occupy. Presumably, the more people draw on their selves to perform their roles within those boundaries, the more stirring are their performances and the more content they are with the fit of the costumes they don. (p. 692)

Furthermore, according to Kahn,

> When a person is engaged, there is the simultaneous employment and expression of a person's "preferred self" in task behaviors that promote connections to work and to others, personal presence (physical, cognitive, and emotional), and active, full role performances. . . . The combination of employing and expressing a person's preferred self yields behaviors that bring alive the relation of self to role. People who are personally engaged keep their selves within a role, without sacrificing one for the other. (p. 700)

Unfortunately, engaged employees are not necessarily the norm in most American organizations. In a series of interviews with Barb Sanford for the *Gallup Management Journal Online*, Curt Coffman, coauthor of *First Break All the Rules* (Buckingham & Coffman, 1999) and *Follow This Path* (Coffman & Gonzalez-Molina, 2002), discusses the responses of more than 3 million employees to Gallup's Q12 survey that measures employee engagement levels (gmj.gallup.com). The results of the survey reveal three distinct levels of engagement among employees: engaged, not engaged, and actively disengaged.

The "engaged" employees are builders. They use their talents, develop productive relationships, and multiply their effectiveness through those relationships. They perform consistently at high levels. They drive innovation and drive their organization forward. The employees that are "not engaged" aren't necessarily negative or positive about the company. They basically take a wait-and-see attitude toward their job, their employer, and their coworkers. They hang back and don't commit themselves.

This brings us to the "actively disengaged" employees—"the cave dwellers." They're "Consistently Against Virtually Everything." We've all worked with an actively disengaged employee who is not just unhappy at work; he acts out that unhappiness. Every day, actively disengaged employees tear down what their engaged coworkers are building. (Sanford, 2002a, p. 1)

The level of employee engagement as measured by the Gallup Q12 survey was shocking. The results of the research indicated that "29% of the workforce is engaged, 55% is not engaged, and 16% is actively disengaged" (Sanford, 2002a, p. 2). Coffman puts it more dramatically: "For every two builders walking the halls of your organization, there is a cave dweller impeding the good work done by the engaged employees. . . . If 55% of all U.S. workers are not engaged, and 16% are actively disengaged, then 71% of the Americans who go to work every day aren't engaged in their role" (Sanford, 2002a, p. 2).

What does this lack of engagement do to productivity? How does low engagement affect the bottom line? Gallup has estimated that actively disengaged workers, those that are the least productive, cost the American economy $350 billion or more annually (Coffman & Gonzalez-Molina, 2002). This figure, of course, doesn't take into account the largest group of workers in the engagement quotient, the disengaged workers, who comprise 55 percent of the workforce and produce much less than they would be capable of producing if they were fully engaged. When taken as a whole, the cost of lost productivity to American business by these large groups of disengaged and actively disengaged workers is staggering.

Coffman (Sanford, 2002b) believes that almost everyone joins an organization as an engaged employee and that what "managers do from that point forward determines the path the employee will take—toward continued engagement or toward the ranks of the 'not engaged' or 'actively disengaged' groups" (p. 1). Coffman, as quoted by Sanford (2003), suggests six strategies that the best managers or leaders can use to help get the maximum productivity (through engagement) out of employees:

1. First, great managers maintain strong, caring relationships with every individual on their teams. They realize that the level of trust between a manager and employee will determine how the employee deals with problems.

2. This leads us to the second strategy: communication. Great managers clearly define and consistently communicate goals and objectives to their team members—and they individualize that communication to unleash each person's potential for performance.

3. They (great managers) can help employees see their connection to customers. Employees drive a customer's attachment to an organization, so every employee has a crucial role to play in helping his organization serve its customers.

4. Next, great managers reinforce those connections to customers—and the importance of each employee's role—through recognition. For them, recognizing employees isn't a "feel-good" issue; it's how the organization communicates its values to employees.

5. Great managers give employees freedom to act. They define the right outcomes, then step aside and let each employee find his own way toward meeting those expectations.

6. Great managers focus on the development of the individual and the team. They use workplace challenges to help their employees grow, because each employee's growth is crucial to increasing the team's value in the organization. (pp. 1–3)

These recommendations appear to me to be strikingly similar to the findings of the Best Employers in Canada study cited earlier (Howe, 2003), and can easily be adapted by school leaders to fit their circumstances.

Clearly, caring is at the heart of achieving and maintaining a high level of employee engagement in the workplace. A good argument could be made that five of the six strategies (and perhaps all six) that Coffman endorses as a means to achieve maximum productivity from employees involve a significant element of caring. To avoid becoming disengaged, employees need to have strong, caring relationships and clear communications with both their leaders and their coworkers. They need to understand their connection to the customer (or client, in the case of schools) and to work in an environment that frees them to take risks and to do their best to meet the expectations of the organization. When those expectations are met, employees need to be recognized for upholding the values of the organization. Finally, employees also need opportunities to continue to develop their talents and abilities and grow in the organization as they continue to strive for excellence in their work. Without question, there is a high degree of caring involved in most, if not all, of these strategies.

By the way, I don't think that it's an accident that Coffman (Sanford, 2003) places "strong, caring relationships" at the head of his list of strategies for achieving the maximum productivity from employees. More and more, the importance of caring to successful leadership is being recognized. For example, Kouzes and Posner in their book *Encouraging the Heart: A Leader's Guide to Rewarding and Recognizing Others* (1999) present a summary of the results of a Center for Creative Leadership study of managerial effectiveness:

Rather, the single factor that differentiated the top from the bottom was higher scores on affection—both expressed and wanted. Contrary to the myth of the cold-hearted boss who cares very little about people's feelings, the highest-performing managers show more warmth and fondness toward others than do the bottom 25 percent. They get closer to people, and they're significantly more open in sharing thoughts about feelings than their lower performing counterparts. (p. 9)

This finding is not unique. There are numerous other examples in the literature over the past fifteen to twenty years from a variety of fields that illustrate the important role caring plays in effective leadership and ultimately in successful organizations (Csikszentmihalyi, 2003; Howe, 2003; Yudd, 2002; Coffman & Gonzalez-Molina, 2002; Thamara, 1994; Suters, 1991).

Traditionally, caring is not a concept that has been all that warmly endorsed by leaders as a key leadership trait in many fields. Rather, until recently, competition has been at the heart of the American system for doing business. The prevailing belief has been that the strong survive and prosper while the weak fall by the wayside. But when it comes to leadership, what qualities denote strong and weak? Mental toughness, power, and aggressiveness have been highly regarded as leadership strengths while other qualities such as sensitivity, communication, and caring have been less valued.

Solomon (1992), however, has suggested that perhaps caring deserves a higher place in the pantheon of leadership traits:

"Caring" is not a word that makes executive hearts beat faster or stronger. It does not get the adrenalin flowing or the muscles flexing the way "competition" and "the profit motive" do. . . . But much of the uninspiring imagery of caring has to do with the overly military and otherwise macho metaphors that have dominated so much of business thinking in this century. . . . Indeed, when one thinks of the "survival of the fittest" imagery applied to the corporation, it becomes obvious that the fittest corporation will be one that cares for and nurtures its employees and managers rather than one that leaves them to fight it out amongst themselves. Nevertheless, caring is too often thought to be too "soft" to be good for business, while internecine squabbling, no matter how destructive, is somehow accepted as a sign of health and strength. Nothing could be further from the truth, or as bad for business. (p. 226)

Goleman, Boyatzis, and McKee (2002) note that, although it has long been suspected that there is a positive link between an organization's climate and its performance, hard data to connect the two have been scarce. This has allowed some leaders to ignore their personal style and focus more on business objectives. But more recent data suggest that this is probably not wise:

But now we have positive results from a range of industries that link leadership to climate and to business performance, making it possible to quantify the hard difference for business performance made by something as soft as the "feel" of a company. . . . In a study of nineteen insurance companies, the climate created by the CEO among their direct reports predicted the business performance of the entire organization: in 75 percent of the cases, climate alone accurately sorted companies into high versus low profits and growth. . . . If climate drives business, what drives climate? Roughly 50 to 70 percent of how employees perceive their organization's climate can be traced to the actions of one person: the leader. More than anyone else, the boss creates the conditions that directly determine people's ability to work well. (pp. 17–18)

If Solomon (1992) and Goleman and colleagues (2002) are right in their conclusions—and I believe that they are—then perhaps the strongest leaders in all kinds of organizations are not necessarily the hardest or the toughest, but rather the most sensitive, caring, gentle, and compassionate.

The title of this chapter poses a question: "Why should leaders care about caring?" I believe the answer to this question is not complicated. Leaders should care about caring because caring is the best resource leaders have at their disposal to build organizations that attract, retain, and develop the most able and talented people available. Caring makes it possible to build organizations where employees are highly motivated to come to work each day, make the best contribution they are capable of making to the mission of the organization, and, ultimately, to improve the organization's bottom line. Caring makes it possible for leaders to build organizations where employees are fully engaged in their work, resulting not only in stronger, more productive organizations, but also in happier, healthier human beings with a better quality of life.

Engaged employees are eleven times more likely than their actively disengaged comrades to indicate that they are extremely satisfied with their current company as a place to work. They are four times more likely to evaluate their condition of life as excellent, and twice as likely to say that they are extremely satisfied with their personal lives. In contrast, actively disengaged employees feel much less confident. They are nine times more likely than engaged employees to say that they are less secure about their jobs than they were a year before. They are three times more likely to indicate that their stress-related work has caused them to behave poorly with their families, and twice as likely to indicate that they have less time to do the things they want to do. (Coffman & Gonzalez-Molina, 2002, pp. 135–136)

If leaders care about caring and actively demonstrate that caring, then others in the organization will care about caring, as well. Employees will be more highly engaged in their work and will care more about the quality of the work that they perform. Because they care, engaged employees will invest more of their physical, cognitive, and mental selves in doing their work well. Engaged employees will care more for their coworkers, their clients, and, ultimately, they will care more about the general welfare and overall success of the organizations that employ them. So what is the definitive answer to the question, "Why should leaders care about caring?" Leaders should care about caring because they are responsible for building winning teams and winning organizations, and these are best built, not by carpenters, but by *carpenters by trade.*

TAKE TIME TO REFLECT

1. Csikszentmihalyi (2003) was quoted in this chapter as saying that "although 80 percent of adults claim that they would continue to work even if they had so much money that they didn't have to worry about having more, the majority can hardly wait each day to leave their job and go home" (p. 86). Do you believe that Csikszentmihalyi is correct? If he is correct, then what do you think are the causes for this large measure of disaffection that adults have for the workplace? Do you think the majority of your colleagues can't wait to leave work each day? Ask some and find out. And if they do, find out why.

2. Think of a time when you were highly engaged in your work. What were the factors that led to that high level of engagement? Were there elements of caring that were readily identifiable in your particular work setting? How did leadership or management communicate caring to you as an individual, as well as to others in the organization?

CHAPTER FIVE

WHAT DO I CARE ABOUT?

Although there are numerous important questions that leaders should be asking themselves, I believe that none is so vital to success in a leadership role as "What do I care about?" Why is this question so critical? It is critical because the things a person cares about define the central core of who that person is as a human being and as a leader. The things we truly care about frame our value system and, as Johnson (2005) reminds us, "Our values serve as a moral compass to guide us on our journey" (p. 81).

If you think about it, what you truly care about will dictate the things you will be passionate about, the things you will fight for, sacrifice for, and in extreme cases, the things you might even be willing to die for. Caring is the central quality that gives human beings a purpose in life—a reason to get up in the morning—even the will to live! I agree with Charles Handy (1989), who makes the point that "care is not a word to be found in many organizational textbooks, or in books on learning theory, but it should be" (p. 232).

I am thoroughly convinced that the things in life that people really care about and the ways in which they express the depths of that caring in daily interactions with others are the chief determinants of whether or not others can and will trust them enough to allow them to lead. Csikszentmihalyi (2003) explains why this is so:

To bring as much flow into one's life as possible, the first step one must take is to define one's priorities—the things one believes are worth living for. . . . A leader will find it difficult to articulate a coherent vision unless it expresses his core values, his basic identity. (p. 167)

We all know people who profess not to care very much about anything, and others who care deeply but whose caring is often focused on the wrong things. Both the words and the actions of people who don't care and those who care about the wrong things give them away. In daily conversations, people who don't care about anything routinely send signals confirming their lack of caring. For example, you might ask them a question such as "Who do you want to win the election?" Their response goes something like this: "It doesn't make any difference; they're all a bunch of crooks anyway." Or you may ask them, "What do you want to see at the movies?" Their response: "It doesn't matter to me; none of them are any good anymore—too much sex and violence." Or you're fixing a sandwich for yourself and your uninspired friend, and you ask, "What would you like on your hamburger?" The non-caring people I am referring to frequently answer with a sad note of resignation in their voices: "I don't really care—just give me the same stuff on mine that you're having on yours."

Don't these people drive you crazy? Aren't they the most depressing human beings on the face of the earth? Wouldn't you like to tell them to "just grow up and get a life"? And wouldn't it be fun to say, "Well I'm having Hershey's chocolate syrup on my hamburger, and I'd be more than happy to spread some on yours!" The problem is that most of the people I'm talking about would probably be just as happy with the chocolate syrup as not. The point is that people who don't care can never be leaders. They have no passion, they have no commitment, they have no capacity to inspire others. A leader can only give away to others the things that he or she already possesses, and we all expect and deserve to receive a great deal from our leaders in terms of passion, inspiration, and commitment.

Lest we forget, there are plenty of people who care, but who care for the wrong things. In the popular motion picture *Jerry Maguire* (Brooks & Scott, 1996), the signature line that jumps out at the audience is, "Show me the money!" This is the "family motto" that the professional football star makes his agent, Jerry Maguire, repeat into the phone before he would agree to sign with him. "Say it, Jerry. Say 'Show me the money!'" It doesn't matter to the star which team will sign him to the big contract, the colors of the team uniforms, or even the city where he will be playing; nothing matters to him except the big payday.

The movie portrays sports agents (even the hero, Jerry Maguire, before he comes to his senses) as ruthless sharks that will do anything to land clients and score a healthy percentage from their clients' lucrative contracts. Key virtues such as love, loyalty, honor, commitment, friendship, devotion, responsibility, and integrity all take a backseat to cold, hard cash in the high-stakes, highly competitive world surrounding the marketing of professional athletes. The primary message of the movie is that, unless we are careful, we can find ourselves living in a cynical world where success is measured in dollars and cents, and where virtues are for losers.

Most of us would agree that it would be very sad indeed if selfishness were the primary motivator for the majority of the people in the world. What would the world be like if nothing mattered except the size of a person's bank account? I don't know about you, but personally I find it reassuring to know that many, if not most, individuals and organizations value a lot of things besides money and the outward trappings that come with financial success. If financial success were all that really mattered in our society, then we wouldn't have so many incredibly talented and capable people and civic-minded companies devoting a large part of their lives and fortunes to goals outside themselves. Csikszentmihalyi (2003) issues a warning to leaders who may not understand that success must ultimately be measured in more than dollars and cents:

> But the way we make a living, the jobs we have, and the way our work is rewarded have a tremendous bearing on our lives, making them either exciting and rewarding, or dull and anxious. For this reason alone anyone in charge of a workplace is obligated to consider the question: How am I contributing to human well-being? (p. 5)

The two things that I have been discussing, a lack of caring and caring about the wrong things, can lead to cynicism in people and in organizations when carried to the extreme. Cynicism is a deadly poison. If left unchecked, it can spread from one person to another like wildfire and geometrically diminish the positive potential to accomplish the most essential and worthwhile goals in any organization.

I, for one, don't want to spend my work life surrounded by cynics. They drain my energy. They drag me down and suck all the joy out of living. I had an acquaintance (cynics can never be real friends to anyone, including themselves) when I was in college whom we all laughingly referred to as the "black cloud." He was certain that behind every silver lining, there must be a black cloud. But just ask him to do something about it, to take an active role in solving a problem, to be personally involved and accountable for making a situation better, and watch him run away as fast as he could. He cared just enough to criticize, but never quite enough to make things better. Wherever he went, it was his mission in life to drag everyone else down to the depths where he resided. From his perspective, nothing was ever as it should be and nothing ever suited him. I believe his two favorite colors must have been black and dark black. When he dies, his epitaph should read, "I told you I was sick!"

People such as the black cloud are sad commentaries on the human condition. They stumble and bumble their way through life, criticizing without caring—expertly pointing out life's problems while deftly avoiding their responsibility to be a part of the solutions. Sad to say, it almost seems as if it is mandated by law that every organization must have a few black clouds with whom they must contend. In fact, black clouds are those actively disengaged workers that were discussed in Chapter 4, those miserable souls who devote their efforts to undermining the positive contributions made to the organization by their actively engaged coworkers. I can't even imagine what daily life in an organization would be like without the customary quota of black clouds, but I would like to find out.

At the opposite extreme from those who don't care about anything or those who care primarily about the wrong things are the people who care a great deal about the right things—in fact, they could even be described as being passionate about the right things. We choose these people as our leaders because their passion reflects our deepest-held values and convictions. Their expressed values represent the things that we see as good and noble in life. Despite the messiness and uncertainties of life, these people have a genuine zest for living. They want to be involved in everything and are willing to experience the defeats as well as the victories. Perhaps more than anything, they want to be insiders rather than outsiders in life: to be active players in the game, to have their lives count for something, and to make a real difference. I love these people! They are precisely the kind of people I want to have in my own life, because I feel and cherish their caring. You can hear caring echoing in the passion of their voices; you can see it reflected in the glint in their eyes. It's both confirming and humanizing for me to be able to identify with the peaks and valleys of their successes and disappointments, victories and defeats; it is energizing for me to be an active player along with others in a worthwhile struggle.

Caring so deeply about something that it can even be described as a passion is critical to effective leadership. Stanford-Blair and Dickmann (2005) conducted a revealing study of thirty-six diverse leaders in terms of culture, gender, and experience in a variety of fields from around the world. These researchers focused their efforts on examining "how leaders are formed to the task of influencing the capacity of others, how they perform such influence, and how they sustain their influence over time" (p. xii). Stanford-Blair and Dickmann found passion to be a key component of the characters of the successful leaders that they studied:

> Humble servants that they professed to be, the 36 leaders nevertheless described themselves as characteristically very aware of and committed to their passions. They were always focusing themselves and those they served in a straightforward manner on important matters that warranted meaningful attention. They were also both tough and vulnerable in their championing of compelling purpose. (p. 66)

Based on my own experiences as a follower, I know why passion expressed as compelling purpose is deeply ingrained in the character of successful leaders. Passionate leaders make me feel alive and vital; they help me appreciate what it's like to be an insider riding the crests of the ebbs and flows of life in pursuit of a compelling purpose. They make me feel as if I matter and that my own caring can make a significant difference in my life and in the lives of others. Perhaps most important, people who care deeply about a compelling purpose make me want to be a better person than I might otherwise be without their connection to my life. Passionate people are exactly the kind of people whom I trust to lead me.

One night, I was sitting in my favorite chair channel surfing, when I clicked to a station where a woman was conducting an interview with the principal of an inner-city elementary school. Apparently, this principal's school was being recognized for its success in promoting high achievement for students from low-income backgrounds. Naturally, the program focused on the characteristics that made this school special—the things that this particular school was doing with and for children that allowed them to be successful despite their difficult economic circumstances.

During the interview, the principal recounted his first year in the school and the difficulties he had experienced coming into and adjusting to the situation. He talked about his first semester in the school and that much-needed first Christmas vacation. He talked about the first day back at school when the students returned from the winter break, and a conversation he had had with a second-grade student. As the principal was making the rounds of the campus, he met the student coming down the hall. The principal greeted the small boy and asked him, "Well Billy, tell me, what did you get for Christmas?" The boy's response was, "Mr. Principal, I didn't get nothing for Christmas."

As the principal related this story, he became emotional. I believe that I might even have seen tears welling up in his eyes. It was both touching and inspiring for me to see this big, strong, important man so moved while discussing the distressing circumstances of a single small child in his school. He cleared his throat and told the interviewer, "At that precise moment, I made a vow to myself that no child in that school would ever again be able to say, 'Mr. Principal, I didn't get nothing for Christmas.'" He then went on to describe how he had organized the businesses in the local community to establish a fund to ensure that every child in his school would have a happy Christmas from that day forward.

I can't tell you precisely what this particular school did to help its low-income students become academically successful, but I can venture a reasonable guess as to the reason. The school was successful because the school leader cared about the children a great deal. Although I didn't see any of the teachers or other staff members interviewed, I can assure you that they cared a great deal about the children as well. I watched the remainder of the interview with keen interest. Here was a guy who was living my deepest beliefs about the benefits of caring to the success of organizations. He summed up his leadership philosophy in a way that reflected his total commitment to helping each individual child. He said that good leaders must understand the law and bureaucracy and the policies that are a direct result of law and bureaucracy. He then added that, if necessary, the good leader will then discard law, bureaucracy, and policies and do what's best for the children.

Now tell me, what parent wouldn't want this man to be the principal of his or her child's school? What teacher wouldn't want to work with a principal who cared so much and demonstrated that caring in such a powerful and compelling way?

I am convinced that if everyone in a school, working together as a cohesive unit, cares enough about the children, then together they will find out what needs to be done to make the children successful and they will do everything in their power to see that it gets done! How can we expect parents to trust and support schools with their precious children unless we who work in those schools can demonstrate beyond all doubt that we genuinely and deeply care about what happens to those children? In other words, both parents and children need to be sure that those of us in schools care a lot about the right things. This is the only way we can gain the trust and support required to be able to lead successfully.

During my time as a school principal, I sat with many parents whose children were experiencing difficulties in school. More than anything else that I could possibly have done for these parents, they wanted and deserved to see some small sign from me that I genuinely cared about their children.

In all the years I've worked in and around schools, I've never been acquainted with a successful leader who didn't care a great deal about the mission of the school and the people who were working with her or him to make that mission a reality. And I've never known a successful school leader who didn't value key virtues such as love, loyalty, honor, commitment, friendship, devotion, responsibility, and integrity above personal gain. The best leaders I've ever been associated with not only cared, but also expressed their caring freely and openly with their colleagues on a daily basis in a hundred different ways. Autry (1991) perhaps says it best: "Good management is largely a matter of love. Or if you're uncomfortable with that word, call it caring, because proper management involves caring for people, not manipulating them" (p. 13). I'm convinced that more than anything else, people want to feel genuine caring from their leaders; in fact, they even demand it if they are to follow.

Organizations cannot survive, much less prosper, with too many people who don't care deeply about the mission and goals of the organization, or too many whose caring is focused on the wrong things. Consequently, leaders must examine their own deepest-held values by constantly asking themselves questions such as "What do I care about?" "What are my core values that I will not compromise under any circumstances? "What kind of person and leader do I want to be?" "What kind of person and leader do I definitely not want to be?" "What should this organization stand for and against?" Leaders must then light the way for others by helping them to identify and embrace their own key values, and by helping them align these values with those of the organization so that they can achieve what Csikszentmihalyi (2003) has termed "flow" in an organizational setting. He uses flow to describe a state where people are in tune with the values of the organization and are functioning at their highest levels of productivity as they are "carried away by an outside force, of moving effortlessly with a current of energy, at the moments of highest enjoyment" (p. 39). Flow can be achieved only in organizations when people come to embrace important organizational values as their own.

I am a person who cares a great deal. I care about things both great and small. I care about whales, and I care about butterflies. I am genuinely concerned about the depletion of the ozone layer, the destruction of the Amazon rain forests, and whether or not the young people who are just starting out in their working lives will be able to support the huge numbers of Baby Boomers who will be retiring in the near future. I worry about whether or not my own children will be responsible adults who are capable of taking care of themselves while caring for others. I also worry that I may not be able to swerve fast enough to avoid squashing that careless squirrel up the street that occasionally darts in front of my car.

Caring is the one defining quality in my life that gives it meaning. Two of my most important goals in life are to care more with each successive day, and to focus that care in the areas that matter most to me. So what do you care about? Do you take time to reflect on the most important things in your own life? Do you ever ask yourself the basic question, "What do I care about?" How do you demonstrate your caring to others who are central in your work and in your personal life? Have you tried to structure your organization in such a way that it supports a caring ethic and provides flow for those whom you are serving in a leadership role? What can you do to help make your life as well as your work environment better reflect the things you really care about?

TAKE TIME TO REFLECT

1. Suppose you had to suddenly give up everything you care about in your life—your relationships with others, your possessions, your values—one thing at a time. What are the relationships, the values, or the possessions you would choose to cling to until the very end? Make a list of the things about which you care deeply (e.g., good health, religion, professional status, personal growth, integrity, financial wealth, family, friends). Put your list in priority order and then compare how much you say you value each item with how much of yourself you devote to nurturing and caring for those things. Is there a pretty good match? If not, what can you do about it?

2. If you are working with a group, brainstorm a list of things that people say they care about (see the question above). After your list is complete, give individuals the opportunity to discuss and even advocate for the items they feel are the most important on the list. Now whittle down the list using an approach that allows the group to reach consensus on the ten or so most important items on the list. What did this process reveal to you about the things human beings value? Was the process of arriving at consensus easier or more difficult than you expected? Are we human beings more similar than we are different, as measured by the things we value?

3. Discuss how the things that you personally care about affect your capacity to lead others. Do you sense a need to reprioritize your system of values? If so, what might change for you?

CHAPTER SIX

WHAT DO I BELIEVE ABOUT PEOPLE?

W hat do you believe about people? How do you treat people in your everyday interactions with them? What do you say about them in your conversations with friends and colleagues? Do you regard people as being essentially good, kind, and caring in their dealings with others, or as evil, mean, and nasty? Do you think of most people as being lazy or industrious? Selfish or giving? Boring or interesting? Dull or ingenious? When you meet someone for the first time, do you automatically size that person up based on the upside or the downside of his or her potential? Are you an optimist or a pessimist when it comes to evaluating the basic worth of other human beings? The answers to these questions are critical: They define your personal personnel philosophy and set the parameters for how you will approach and work with others in a leadership role, as well as how others will be inclined to respond to your attempts to lead.

Margaret Wheatley (2005) expresses the opinion that "Western cultural views of how best to organize and lead (the majority paradigm in use in the world) are contrary to what life teaches" (p. 1). Wheatley is distressed by what she regards as leaders' feeble attempts to lead through the imposition and tightening of controls in order to get people to comply with their leadership demands rather than through the engagement of their best capacities by working with them as partners. According to Wheatley,

Leaders use primitive emotions of fear, scarcity, and self-interest to get people to do their work, rather than the more noble human traits of cooperation, caring and generosity. This has led us to a difficult time, when nothing seems to work as we want it to, when too many of us feel frustrated, disengaged and anxious. (p. 2)

I believe that Wheatley has a valid point. Based on my own leadership studies, observations of others, and personal experiences in a variety of leadership roles over many years, it seems clear to me that attempts by leaders to exercise tight control over people can never lead to the absolute best possible outcomes for any organization. Human nature simply won't allow this to happen, because human beings have free will and they will resist moving in any direction that is not consistent with their own beliefs and values. Put another way, *no organization is going anywhere that the people who make up the organization don't want it to go.*

I am convinced that leaders' attempts to lead are based primarily on what they believe about people. If leaders believe that people are essentially honest, hardworking, responsible, committed, creative, talented, and capable, then they will treat them as partners and give them the opportunity and the freedom to become the best that they can be in an organization. If leaders believe the reverse to be true, then they will try everything in their power to tightly structure and control how their people function in the workplace. Sad to say, leaders who seek to tightly control other human beings are doomed to failure.

It is one of the great ironies of our age that we created organizations to constrain our problematic human natures, and now the only thing that can save these organizations is a full appreciation of the expansive capacities of us humans. (Wheatley, 2005, p. 21)

A few years ago, one of my colleagues offered me the opportunity to go to a medium-security prison and conduct some sessions on personal awareness with the inmates. Now, I freely admit that at first I wasn't all that excited about the opportunity. This was a voluntary activity for me and for the prisoners. If I accepted the invitation, then I would be expected to go into the prison and give my time and energy to a group of men who had done some pretty awful things, or they wouldn't have landed in prison in the first place.

In all honesty, I felt that I had very little in common that I could share with the prisoners. My instincts told me that if I were the least bit intelligent, I would avoid putting myself in such an uncomfortable situation. I was afraid that, because I came from a world that was foreign to the one in which they lived, the prisoners wouldn't be able to relate to me at all, or perhaps I would be intimidated by them, or perhaps they would reject me and my ideas and leave me feeling embarrassed and inadequate.

Acting against my instincts, I accepted the challenge to go and work with the inmates. And guess what happened? To my surprise and relief, none of the unpleasant things occurred that I had imagined. The prisoners came into the meeting room at the appointed time. They took their seats in a large circle and listened intently as I explained my goals for the activities I had planned for the session that afternoon. When I talked, they were attentive; when I asked questions, they gave thoughtful responses; when I asked them to engage in a series of activities, they willingly participated. As they interacted with each other, they were surprisingly polite and respectful of the attitudes and opinions of others. To say that I was impressed by their behavior would be a gross understatement: I was astounded!

When I had finished my planned activities with the prisoners, they invited me to take part in a little reception they had arranged, complete with refreshments. As we milled about the meeting room enjoying our punch and cookies and chatting about one thing and another, I felt as if I had suddenly been transported to the "twilight zone." Just a few short hours before, I could not have imagined myself sharing punch and cookies and conversation with a room full of convicted felons. As we talked, I learned that the men who were pleasantly socializing all around me were incarcerated for a variety of serious crimes. Some of them were serving life sentences for murder, and others were doing time for rape or armed robbery or some other heinous misdeed. What was incredible to me when I reflected on the experience later was that if I had not had knowledge of who these men were and why they were there, I would never have known that they were capable of doing some of the awful things that they had done. It almost scares me to admit it, but in many fundamental respects, these men were exactly like you and me.

Clearly, I had grossly underestimated the inmates' potential as human beings, and relied instead on the stereotypes that I held about criminals to shape my attitudes prior to my up-close and personal experience with those men that day. Regardless of what else they were, they were first and foremost human beings. They had many of the same hopes, fears, and dreams that we all do. They loved their families; they suffered feelings of guilt; they regretted the actions that had irreparably damaged their lives. On reflection, I was forced to admit to myself, given a different set of circumstances, they might have been in my place and I might have been in theirs.

This is my long-winded way of saying that we all have the potential to be a lot of things in life. In a way, the line between self-belief and self-doubt creates a prison for all of us. Leaders have a responsibility to find ways to open the doors of those self-imposed prisons and let hearts and minds soar to new heights. I suppose it would be pushing a point for me to say that we as leaders are capable of turning our fellow human beings into people who may be quite different from the persons they might otherwise have become. But in my view, it is critical for leaders to believe that there is a world of good to be found in every human being. A leader's beliefs will shape the way in which he or she will interact with others, and, in the end, impose limits or grant freedoms so that a person can become the best or the worst that she or he is capable of becoming. As Welch (2005) has reminded all those who would lead, "Before you are a leader, success is all about growing yourself. When you become a leader, success is all about growing others" (p. 61).

I try to shape my interactions with others through a set of beliefs that mirror my faith in the fundamental decency and goodness of people. These few beliefs, which I refer to as my personal personnel philosophy, are simple, but they have served me well over many years.

First, I believe that most people are basically good and kind and caring. I believe that people are industrious, giving, interesting, and ingenious. I am quite sure that almost every person I have ever known is capable of the very best or the very worst in humankind and that it is my responsibility as a leader to find ways to free them to discover the best person that they can be in an organizational setting. De Pree (1989) reminds leaders that "people need to be liberated, to be involved, to be accountable, and to reach for their potential" (p. 97).

I believe that it is not just the individual alone, making decisions and acting on those decisions, who determines what he or she can or will accomplish in an organization, but also the attitudes of others and the resulting circumstances that are an outgrowth of those attitudes. Therefore, as a leader I have a responsibility to reflect the kind of positive attitudes and caring toward my colleagues that will help shape the circumstances that promote personal growth and satisfaction for all of us working and living together in the organization.

Perhaps the most important component of my personal personnel philosophy is the belief that every individual in an organization wants to do a good job. In all my years of working in leadership roles, I've never had anyone tell me or otherwise indicate by act or deed that he or she wanted to perform poorly in his or her job. I simply can't believe that anyone goes home from a job and says, "I just love being awful at my job!" When I tell some people that I believe that everyone wants to do a good job, they laugh and tell me I must be a complete fool, because they know a lot of people who clearly don't want to do a good job. To this, my stock reply is, "I would rather be a fool than a cynic!" Cynics are deadly in an organizational setting. They have abandoned all hope and can never expect things to be appreciably better than they are presently or than they used to be.

The simple truth is that when a leader is seeking to discover the nature of human beings, most times that leader will find exactly what she or he is looking for. That's why it's essential for me to believe that everyone wants to do a good job. If you believe that most people are lazy and don't care enough to expend the time and energy required for them to perform their jobs at a high level, then you will find ample evidence to support this conclusion. Everywhere you look in your organization, you will find lazy, careless, incompetent people trying to beat the system, intent on giving as little as possible while taking as much from the organization as they can get away with. On the other hand, if you believe that everyone wants to do a good job and that each person will rise to the challenge and exert as much time and energy as is required to get the job done in a professional and caring manner, you will find just as much evidence to support this conclusion. I know that I have seen many teachers, counselors, principals, and others who have struggled early in their job tenures, but who later on, through hard work and commitment (both on their own part and on their leader's part), turned out to be extraordinary performers.

This is not to say that everyone in an organization is doing a good job. To believe that is true would indeed be foolish. There are any number of individuals in most organizations who, for one reason or another, may not be doing a good job. They may not have the skills they need to be able to perform key tasks, or perhaps they do not have the requisite knowledge central to doing their jobs well. In other circumstances, people may not be sufficiently motivated to perform well, or the work setting may not be organized in such a way that it allows them to be successful in their efforts to perform at a high level. In certain instances, we may be asking someone to do the impossible by placing them in a work environment where even the most capable and competent individual might not be able to succeed. For example, a principal may give a first-year teacher a teaching assignment comprising a combination first-grade and kindergarten class of remedial learners. The point is that there are many reasons outside an individual's desire to do a good job that may negatively affect one's job performance. This leads to the next tenet of my personal personnel philosophy: Everyone can do a good job given the proper support and assistance.

One spring while I was an undergraduate student, I took a civil service examination and qualified for a summer job at the post office. I was excited about the opportunity because I had never held a job that paid above the minimum wage. The only downside to this job was that it was in a neighboring city about thirty-five miles from where I was living at the time. The distance wasn't so much of a problem as was my unfamiliarity with the city where I would be working. People who know me well will tell you that I have a terrible sense of direction. A number of my friends go so far as to claim that I am "directionally disabled." Knowing this, my chief concern with my new job was whether or not I would be able to find my way around in a strange city well enough to perform the job satisfactorily. After all, I really wanted to do a good job.

When I arrived at the post office that first day to begin my job, my supervisor, a grizzled, veteran postal worker, taught me the ropes. He showed me where to get the mail that I would be delivering on my semirural route. He showed me how to sequence the individual pieces of mail to correspond with the route I would be following during delivery, and then he took me with him in the mail truck while he drove the route and we delivered the day's mail. Thinking back on the experience, I remember that first day as a blur. Every aspect of the job—the rules, the regulations, the procedures—was all new to me. I remember being dazed by information overload. And, to make matters worse, I was directionally disabled!

When I showed up for work the next day, my anxiety level was at a near-record high. On that second day, there was no grizzled veteran ready to take me through my paces. It was my responsibility, and my responsibility alone, to get the job done. I went to the window where I had been instructed to pick up the mail for my route, received it from the clerk, and carefully began sorting it by the street addresses that were about as familiar to me as downtown Cairo, Egypt. It took me what seemed like forty forevers just to sequence the mail for delivery. By the time I had finished this preliminary chore, the other postal workers had long since departed to begin delivering their mail. At long last, I finished the mail sorting and climbed into my assigned vehicle to make my deliveries.

The first few streets on my route were close to the post office and easy enough for me to remember. I delivered a tray or two of mail at a couple of small businesses and emptied two red and blue mail drops into large, white, canvas sacks to take back to the post office with me later that afternoon. I did one or two more streets; then the world closed in on me! I was lost. I couldn't remember where to go next. The city map unfolded on the truck seat next to me didn't seem to correspond at all to the patchwork of blacktop two-lane highways and dirt roads that I was wandering over aimlessly in my big, white, government vehicle.

The upshot of all this is that not much mail got delivered on my route that day. Most of the people on my route must have thought it was a government holiday when they checked their mailboxes that afternoon. Thank goodness I was finally able to find the post office and park my truck. It was well after dark, and I had spent almost ten hours trying but failing to do what was designed as a six-hour job. I am not exaggerating one bit when I tell you that I took back more mail to the post office that day than I had delivered. I had the mail I had retrieved from the drop boxes and about two-thirds of the mail I had set out to deliver that morning! I felt like a miserable failure! I *was* a miserable failure!

I slunk into the post office and found the supervisor who had attempted to train me the day before. He was busy at some routine task. I walked straight up to where he was working and told him point blank, "I quit!" He looked up at me from his work, and I'll never forget his cryptic response: "Son, nobody quits a government job!"

It took more than a little reassurance from him before I retracted my resignation and agreed to try again. The next morning, my supervisor again took me through the paces. This time, however, he did it in a more caring and considerate way. He asked me questions to make sure I understood what he was telling me, and he had me ask him questions to show that I understood his instructions. When we went out in the truck to deliver the mail on the route that day, he didn't assume that I knew my way around the area: he pointed out landmarks and had me write key directions on a yellow legal pad. When we left the post office to begin the route, he brought along several indelible markers to write street numbers and names on quite a few of the mailboxes along the route that had previously had no identifying markings whatsoever. It required considerably longer than the six hours the route was supposed to require, but eventually we made it around the entire circuit. To my surprise, when we were done that evening, I had a pretty good picture in my head and on my yellow legal pad of the job that I was supposed to do.

The next day, I again was expected to do the route by myself. This time, however, my supervisor stopped by where I was sorting the mail to check on me, to reassure me, and to answer any last-minute questions that I might have. He also gave me a phone number and told me to give him a call if I got into trouble on the route. When I left the post office that day to begin my route, I felt much more confident than I had two days before. I felt as if I had enough information to do what I needed to do reasonably well, and I knew that, in a pinch, I could call on my supervisor for support and assistance if I needed it. It took me about two or three hours more than the six normally allocated to deliver the mail that day, but I got the job done. I got every single piece of mail delivered!

When I returned to the post office, I walked in with my head held high. I felt like a success! I *was* a success! Within a few short weeks, I could easily perform my job in the six hours allocated. In fact, I became so proficient that I could do the entire mail route in four hours, and sometimes less. When I began returning to the post office well before I was scheduled to return, I got my second lesson in government employment. Some of my fellow postal workers politely reminded me that my route was a six-hour route and should require a full six hours. As I recall, the way they put it was, "Hey, college boy—that's a six-hour route you're running. We're still going to be delivering the mail on that route after you've gone back to school. Don't you dare come back to this post office in less than six hours!"

I got the message loud and clear! From that point until the end of the summer when my job ended, I would go out on my route, finish most of my work for the expected six-hour day in about three hours, and then take a leisurely two-hour lunch while reading the current issues of many of my favorite magazines that I would then subsequently deliver later in the afternoon to the subscribers on my route. I can't describe how good it felt for me to be able to perform my job well when I had come so close to walking away from it in total disgrace.

I've often wondered what would have happened if my supervisor had let me quit my job at the post office that summer so many years ago. What if he had not had enough confidence in me to encourage me to try again? I would have walked out the door feeling like a failure after my second day on the job. What if he had not taken his job as a supervisor seriously? What if he had not assumed his responsibility to help me succeed? Without question, I would have been a total and complete failure! But fortunately for me, he did take his responsibility as a supervisor seriously, and he did see the potential in me to get the job done. The result was that the job did get done, and if I do say so myself, it got done in an exemplary manner! More important, I felt validated and confident that I could succeed in other situations that might challenge my resourcefulness and resilience in the future. Because of the leadership exercised by my supervisor, I grew as an employee and a person. Perhaps most significant, this experience helped me to realize my responsibility as a leader, to always look for the best in others, to be sensitive to their needs in the workplace, and to do everything in my power to help others realize their potential as responsible employees and as caring human beings.

This brings me to the final tenet of my personal personnel philosophy: It is the organization's responsibility and that of the leader acting on behalf of the organization to provide the necessary support and assistance required for every person in the organization to be successful. As Welch (2005) cautions those who would lead, "Remember, when you were made a leader you weren't given a crown, you were given a responsibility to bring out the best in others" (p. 72).

I am convinced that our basic beliefs about people define the limits of their potential in the workplace. Our positive beliefs about the essential goodness of people give those whom we lead the freedom to do great things; our negative beliefs predispose them to do awful things. Our basic beliefs about people encourage them to succeed on a grand scale or discourage them so that they fail miserably. Our beliefs about people give them license to become the best or the worst that they are capable of becoming. Kouzes and Posner (1999) have put it this way: "Over and over again, they [leaders] express their belief in the innate goodness of human beings. All the energies of the best leaders—in fact, their entire lives—are dedicated to helping people achieve their full potential" (p. 21).

What do you believe about people? How do you communicate those beliefs in an organizational setting? How many people in your organization are struggling every day as they try vainly to meet the expectations attached to their work? What are you doing to help them in their attempts to do a good job? And finally, are you willing to dedicate yourself as a leader to helping people achieve their full potential?

I think that all true leadership is indeed spiritual leadership, even if you hardly ever hear it put that flatly. The reason is that beyond everything else that can be said about it, leadership is concerned with bringing out the best in people. As such, one's best is tied intimately to one's deepest sense of oneself, to one's spirit. My leadership efforts must touch that in myself and in others. (Vaill, 1989, p. 224)

TAKE TIME TO REFLECT

1. So what do you believe about people? What are the basic tenets of your personal personnel philosophy? Take a few moments to think about your beliefs about people and outline your personal personnel philosophy.

2. Our fundamental beliefs about people serve as an underpinning for our behavior in dealing with others in the role of leader. Discuss a time when your negative or positive attitude toward someone affected you in relation to making a decision about him or her. What was the result? Would you do things differently today?

3. We all know stories of people who have come from very difficult backgrounds or those who have serious mental or physical disabilities yet overcame those circumstances to become happy and productive human beings. There are many who believe that the key ingredient that allowed these people to persist and overcome their particular life challenges was that they all had at least one person in their lives who genuinely believed in them, cared about them, and encouraged them not to give up. Do you agree or disagree with this supposition? Why or why not? Has there been someone in your past whose faith in you has helped you overcome the obstacles in your life to become the person you are today? Who was that person and how did they demonstrate their belief in you? If you are working in a group, share your stories with others, if you are comfortable doing so.

CHAPTER SEVEN

AM I TAKING CARE OF
MY WATER BUFFALO?

W hat gives some of us the right to lead and others the responsibility to follow? What are the costs and rewards of leadership and of "followership"? What is the responsibility of leaders to demonstrate caring and compassion for those who dutifully and willingly follow their lead? How can this best be done? How well have you taken care of those whom you have led?

One of the greatest experiences of my life was spending a year in the Philippines as a Fulbright Scholar during the mid-1980s. Many of my experiences there made the year remarkable. Most people would consider the majority of those experiences to be insignificant if taken individually, but together they added up to what was a life-altering experience for me.

During my time in the Philippines, I was reminded of some things that I had conveniently forgotten. For example, I was reminded of what a privilege and stroke of good fortune it was for me to have been born an American citizen. My American citizenship has bestowed on me many rights and privileges that people in other places only dream about. Not the least of these rights is the right to a free and appropriate education, which made it possible for me to become a Fulbright Scholar in the first place.

I was also reminded that, although I have enjoyed all the rights and privileges of American citizenship throughout my lifetime, I have personally done little to earn this incredible birthright. The rights and privileges of my

American heritage are the legacy of countless, nameless, and faceless others who have gone before me, dedicated and courageous men and women who have struggled and suffered and sacrificed to build a free nation, where every man and woman is indeed created equal, and every individual is guaranteed the right to life, liberty, and the pursuit of happiness.

I know it sounds corny, but being born or naturalized as an American citizen is just about the most fortunate single event that can happen in anyone's life. It's too bad that it takes an unusual circumstance like living in a foreign country to be reminded of this simple truth. Since I returned from the Philippines more than twenty years ago, I have kept my passport in my top drawer so I can see it and be reminded of how fortunate I am to be an American every morning when I get a clean pair of socks.

In addition to being reminded of some important things that I had conveniently forgotten, I learned some other valuable lessons while I was in the Philippines. I learned, for example, that although people in different parts of the world may have different customs and habits, we are pretty much the same everywhere. The most basic hopes, dreams, and fears of humans are universal. No matter if people live their lives in the Far East, Africa, or the midwestern United States, mothers and fathers love their children more than they value their own lives, they worry endlessly about their ability to provide secure futures for them, and they struggle to provide them with opportunities to build better lives than the ones they have lived.

Perhaps the best thing about my extended stay in the Philippines was that it gave me an opportunity to slow down a little in a culture where the pace of life is much more relaxed and deliberate than it is in the United States. I found the slower pace frustrating at first, but revitalizing and revealing once I adjusted to it. For the first time in years, I had time to take a deep breath, to think, and to observe the people and events that swirled around me. That's exactly what I was doing one day when a seemingly insignificant event provided me with what I have come to regard as an important insight for those who wish to become outstanding leaders.

I was leaning against the twisted trunk of an old coconut tree, waiting in the shade for the bus to Makati, where I lived with my family at the time. Buses in Metro Manila don't run on any particular schedule: They come when they come. I was fully prepared to wait for two minutes or two hours. After six months in the Philippines, I was finally beginning to master the art of waiting.

Across the road from the bus stop where I waited, a farmer and a *carabao* were plowing a rice paddy in the blazing noonday sun. In the Philippines, carabao, or water buffalo as they are commonly known, are sometimes referred to as Filipino tractors because they are the only available alternative to mechanical farming devices in a largely undeveloped country.

As I watched, the ponderous beast rhythmically swung his head from side to side as he plodded along in knee-deep mud, straining against the weight of an ancient wooden plow. A small, wrinkled, brown-skinned farmer, barefoot and stripped to the waist, balanced precariously on the inclined sides of the rice paddy while skillfully steering the plow behind the slow-moving water buffalo. Down the east side of the small, square rice paddy, the two creatures moved in perfect unison. They turned west, then south, then north, and then west again, finally completing a circuit. When they had traveled the perimeter of the square in this manner several times, the water buffalo stopped dead in his tracks with no apparent sign from the farmer. The farmer jumped nimbly down into the rice paddy near the animal's head and, with the flat of his right foot, splashed cooling water against the great beast's sides. The brown-skinned little man moved deliberately up and down both sides of the panting animal, stopping only to repeat the splashing motion with first one foot, then the other. If a water buffalo can smile, then this one did: he clearly relished his brief respite from the stifling heat and his arduous labor.

I watched with interest as this scenario was repeated numerous times—the animal using his massive strength to pull the plow, the farmer agilely guiding it to where he needed it to go. The steady rhythm of the two creatures spinning out smaller and smaller circuits within the perimeter of the rice paddy was interrupted only by an occasional stop for the frail little man to splash the cooling water on his Filipino tractor. In a few weeks, young green rice plants would be waving in the soft, warm, tropical breezes, and after a time there would be food for another year.

Transfixed, I stood and watched as the man and the animal worked together in this way. The perfect symbiosis represented by the farmer and the water buffalo, each contributing what he was capable of contributing to a common and essential task, created a simple but powerful image. Clearly, it would have been impossible for the farmer to pull the plow or for the great beast to steer it where it needed to go. Each had to play the role for which he was uniquely suited or the task could not be done and, ultimately, there would be no life-sustaining food for either of them.

As we work and play and love our way through life, we find ourselves in so many different roles in our relationships with others. Sometimes it is our lot to pull the plow, to labor and strain against the harness to get to where we need to go. When we are struggling, mired up to our knees in the rich, thick mud of life, we pray that those who guide the plow will recognize and appreciate our efforts and demonstrate appropriate care and concern, much as the farmer did for the water buffalo. When it is our turn to guide the plow, we must likewise be sensitive to the needs of those whose lot it is to pull it and show our appreciation and compassion in ways both great and small. Only in this way can we hope to live well, accomplish much, and retain our humanity.

For the most part, it is classroom teachers who pull the plows on the front lines of the educational enterprise. Day after day, our teachers are mired up to their knees in the rich, thick mud of helping children acquire the knowledge and build the skills that they will need to live successful and rewarding lives. But this is not always the case. Sometimes, those closest to the work are the ones who must guide the plow, and others (administrators, support staff, or perhaps even board members) must display their willingness to take their turn in the harness as appropriate. It's not all that important who pulls or who guides the plow. What is important is that we all work together to make the very best contribution to our common enterprise that we are capable of making and that each of us recognizes, appreciates, and acknowledges the importance of the contributions that others are making to our common mission.

There are no unimportant or insignificant jobs in any organization. Anyone who hopes to lead effectively must recognize the essential truth of this statement and accord the proper respect, dignity, and care to every individual in the organization no matter what his or her station may be in the hierarchy. In fact, in some important respects, there should be no hierarchies in organizations. Rather, in place of a hierarchy, there should be a collection of colleagues dedicated and committed to a common set of values, working together to accomplish the goals that can make those values come to life. Bennis and Goldsmith (2003) have expressed the importance of what I would describe as a form of egalitarian leadership that seems very appropriate for any organization:

> They [leaders] require everyone to participate in leadership—and "followership" as well. These leaders bring diverse talents, perspectives and constituencies together to form an integrated, dynamic whole. They do not stand above those who follow, but stand with them. They are leaders who listen, empower others, generate trust, build relationships, negotiate collaboratively, and resolve conflicts. They are leaders who are able to follow and let others lead. (p. 6)

As a leader, how well are you taking care of your water buffalo? Are you standing with rather than above those who follow? Do you understand the interdependence that binds every single person in an organization to every other person in that organization? Do you freely and frequently acknowledge that interdependence? Do you trust your colleagues enough to give up the reins and let others guide the plow when it is appropriate to do so? Do you feel honored and gratified when you have an opportunity to pull the plow rather than to guide it?

The bus to Makati came and went that day, and still I waited in the shade of the coconut tree and watched the farmer and the water buffalo play out the same scenario over and over again. I was finally learning how to appreciate and even to enjoy the waiting.

TAKE TIME TO REFLECT

1. What are some of the techniques that you presently use to "splash cooling water" on your colleagues in the workplace? Can you think of others that you might use?

2. Brainstorm with your study group (if you are working in a group, or others from your organization if you are not) a list of ways that could be used to recognize and demonstrate appreciation for the contributions of various individuals to the well-being and success of your school or other organization. Select several of these techniques and use them in carrying out your leadership responsibilities. After a few weeks have passed, meet with those with whom you are working to assess the impact of your efforts.

CHAPTER EIGHT

WHAT DOES IT MEAN TO BE A TEACHER?

When I landed my first job as a teacher, I was one of two first-year teachers hired to teach in the school that year. Because I was a new teacher and the school was small and rural, my teaching assignment was challenging, to say the least. I was assigned to teach seventh-, eighth-, ninth-, and tenth-grade English, with an additional assignment of teaching reading to all the seventh- and eighth-grade students who were two or more years below grade level in reading. There weren't enough classrooms for all the teachers in the school, so I had the additional challenge of being designated as a floating teacher, required to travel from classroom to classroom during the course of the day to meet my students.

Unfortunately, there were no empty classrooms available for two of my English classes, and consequently those two classes were assigned to meet in the auditorium. There were no blackboards or lapboards for our use, and the auditorium wasn't heated. The fact that the auditorium wasn't heated may not seem like a big problem for a school located in Florida, but I can tell you from experience that it gets cold in north Florida in the winter in an unheated auditorium. On the coldest days, I would move my classes outside to the football stadium, where the kids could usually find a place out of the wind while taking full advantage of the warm sunshine.

I will never forget what those first few weeks and months of teaching were like. There I was, a first-year teacher with five different preparations, floating

58

from classroom to classroom, and teaching two periods in an unheated auditorium with nothing on which to write. My principal had also scheduled me for first-period planning and assigned me to a desk in the main office area. Looking back, I suppose I was pretty naive, because it took me the better part of a month to realize that the principal had assigned me for that planning time in the office so that he could conveniently dispatch me to cover the first-period classes of teachers who arrived late to school or called in sick at the last minute. As I remember it, I didn't take advantage of too many planning periods during my first semester as a teacher.

The icing on the cake during that first year was my sixth-period reading class that comprised forty-two seventh and eighth graders who were two or more years below grade level in reading. There were only twenty-six desks in Mrs. Peterson's classroom, where I was assigned to teach my reading students. I had all the desks filled with students; two students were assigned to sit in each of the three window boxes, and the rest were scattered about on the floor at my feet. I remember how much I wished that I had had some training in how to teach reading or at least some appropriate materials that I could use with the class.

It was plain bad luck that Lester was a member of my sixth-period reading class as well as a member of my eighth-grade English class, which met earlier in the day. I can still see Lester's face if I close my eyes and concentrate. He bore a strong physical resemblance to the character Zero in the Beetle Bailey comic strips. But compared to Lester, Zero was a near genius. I have often asked myself, "Did Lester really have it in for me, or was he simply a stone-age ADD kid?" Whatever the case, Lester made my life miserable each and every school day.

After numerous referrals to the office, Lester was finally suspended from school, and the assistant principal arranged for Lester's mother to come in for a parent conference. That conference was an epiphany for me! When we had taken our respective seats for the conference, the first words out of Lester's mother's mouth were, "If you people can't handle Lester here at school, then how in the hell do you expect me to handle him at home?" Although I was temporarily stunned by her words, it was at that moment that I knew that this "teaching thing" was going to be a lot more difficult than I had ever imagined it would be.

If I live to be a very old man with a long white beard, I will never forget what those first weeks and months of teaching were like! I will always remember just how ill prepared I was to meet the challenges that went hand in hand with being a new teacher, how isolated I was from my colleagues, how inadequate I felt every day I walked into that little rural schoolhouse to try to teach my students. And I will certainly never forget how insensitive, uncaring, and unprofessional my school leader was to give me a teaching assignment that would have defeated a much more seasoned teacher. I vowed then that if I ever had the opportunity to lead a school, I would make sure that no teacher in my school would ever experience what I experienced those first few weeks and months as a teacher. I can assure you, I have kept that promise.

School leaders must never forget that teaching is the real business of schools, and they must always hold close to their hearts what it means to be a teacher. I find it distressing that the general public has little understanding or respect for what it means to be a teacher, but I find it devastating for school leaders to fail to realize or to forget the high level of sacrifice, dedication, and commitment required to be an effective classroom teacher. Apart from all those first-year teachers who are bound to struggle while they are learning to be teachers, there are all those veteran teachers who grind it out day after day to serve their students' needs to the best of their ability. For example, there is that English teacher who assigns multiple writing experiences for her students and spends hours at night and on weekends grading the assignments and writing feedback to her students. And there is the advanced placement history teacher who has to fight hard for every single dime he needs to buy supplemental texts for his students. And leaders must not forget teachers who are also parents themselves and committed to attending their own children's open houses, football or soccer games, plays, or musical performances, or those teachers who seek to restore the balance in their own lives by participating in hobbies such as theater, or volunteering for service roles in community affairs or charitable organizations.

Teachers, by the way, are among the most highly represented occupational groups in volunteer community organizations and activities. It is not unusual for an average teacher to spend about twelve hours a day, in and out of the classroom, on activities directly related to teaching and school and then actively volunteer time to serve volunteer roles in the community. When I was preparing to write this book, I made the mistake of describing caring teachers to a colleague in terms that she did not appreciate. I described caring teachers as

> the ones who volunteer when there is something to be done and no one wants to do it . . . the ones who come to school early and leave late. . . . Their chief concern is not with taking care of their own personal needs, but with doing more for others.

My colleague, who had devoted most of her professional life to teaching, jumped down my throat. She verbally slammed me to the floor and wouldn't let me up until I cried uncle. I've never heard a more eloquent description of the demands on the life of a caring and committed professional teacher and I wish I could share it with everyone who cares about teachers and teaching:

> You have described a person who does not have a balanced life, or who is single and has nothing else to do. I know this teacher all too well—I am she. I went to school at 6:00 a.m. and stayed until 5:00 p.m., and then came back at night for PTA. I was the main liaison with parents for the school. I was chair of most schoolwide committees. I took the lead in writing curriculum. I was a successful grantwriter. . . . Beginning in 1982, I led the restructuring efforts, not just for my school, but for the entire district. I was a mentor teacher to new and marginal teachers. I made sure that if one of my 150 students was in any school event—athletic or other performance—I attended the performance and made a point of commenting on it to the student in class the next day. I was assistant principal for curriculum and instruction for two years, but it involved even more "extra duty" and took me away from the teaching and interaction with students that I so dearly loved. So I asked for a classroom assignment again. Education was (and is) my passion! I was acknowledged by the school board, administration, parents, and teachers alike as the consummate professional. And I did this while raising four children (the last of whom is sixteen and a senior in high school) and being there for my husband, who spent the last eleven years of his life in a constant battle with lymphoma. I loved teaching, and I wouldn't give up a day of my teaching experience—but I would *never* [italics in original] do it again.
>
> When you care that much, teaching can suck up every minute of your life and still demand more. I definitely did not lead a balanced life, and in my commitment to meet the needs of everyone else in my life, there was no time to ever meet my own needs. In looking back on my career and wondering if my efforts mattered, I feel somewhat like Simón Bolívar, who, on his deathbed, was asked to look back on his life and reflect on how he felt about all he had done for his people. Bolívar responded that he felt like he had been plowing the ocean. . . . Still, I have no regrets; life is about making choices, and I found gratification and fulfillment in how I chose to spend my time in my first career. (Personal communication, November 1998)

I want to take this opportunity to thank my colleague for setting me straight in terms of what it means to be a caring teacher. And I want to thank her for reminding me that there are countless teachers out there who give everything they have for their students every single day they walk into a classroom—and still, the profession demands that they give even more. She forced me to realize that when teachers care too much for their schools and their students, school leaders must occasionally protect them from themselves!

As I related in Chapter 6, I spent a year in the Philippines as a Fulbright Fellow in the mid-1980s. When I returned to my job in the United States, I was asked to write a piece about my experiences in Asia for the departmental newsletter. I can still remember how grateful I felt to be an American citizen and how aware my experiences in the Philippines had made me of the power that education holds to improve the quality of a person's life. I remember that I was more proud than I had ever been before to be a teacher with the opportunity to touch others on a daily basis and to help change lives for the better. These feelings led me to write the following words for our newsletter:

> Teaching is without a doubt the greatest of the helping professions. While it's true that a competent physician can heal a broken bone, a skilled attorney can conjure up a sound argument for a suspended sentence. A man of the cloth can give one hope—if not for this life—at least for a life to come. All these things are wonderful and beautiful in their own right. But a good teacher! A good teacher can give a child power over his or her own life. To me this is infinitely more wonderful and more beautiful.

Do you remember what it was like to be a beginning teacher? If you're not presently a teacher, do you remember what it was like to be one? Do you still recognize and appreciate the incredible demands that come with being a highly committed and caring teacher? Do you know highly committed and caring teachers in your own schools like the one my colleague described? Are you doing everything in your power not only to appreciate them, but also to save them from themselves if need be? School leaders can forget a lot of things, but they must never forget what it means to be a teacher.

TAKE TIME TO REFLECT

1. Do you have vivid memories of your first year as a teacher? What was that experience like for you? If you could go back and alter that experience in some way, how would you make it different? If you could wave a magic wand and make three wishes to improve the first-year teaching experience for others, what would those wishes be?

2. If you are not presently in a teaching role, interview a group of practicing teachers. Ask them what teaching means to them. Ask them what they enjoy most about teaching and what, if anything, distresses them. Ask them how their teaching lives could be made more satisfying and what might be done to make that happen. Arrange with someone in the group for you to have the opportunity to guest teach or team teach a class or two to refresh your memory of what it means to be a teacher.

CHAPTER NINE

AM I WILLING TO SHARE POWER?

Have you ever felt that the decision-making process in your school or organization was a game? If you felt that the decision-making process was a game, were you also pretty sure that the winners and losers in the game were predetermined? Which side of the game were you on—the winning side or the losing side—and how did it make you feel? As a leader, do you trust others enough to let them in the game? Should the making of important decisions be treated like a game? Can caring be demonstrated by leaders through the way in which important decisions get made?

When I first became the principal of a high school more than thirty years ago, I was shocked when I discovered that the rest of the people in the school didn't seem to me to care as much as I did. This declaration doesn't mean exactly what you might think it does. When I say that others in the school didn't seem to care as much as I did, I'm not being totally fair: The standards I was using to judge caring were so superficial as to be pretty much meaningless. I was equating caring in direct proportion to the staff's willingness to perform additional tasks outside their normal work responsibilities, such as sponsoring activities for students, serving on committees, and performing standing duties. For some reason or reasons unknown to me, the staff members in my school were not eager to assume these added responsibilities, and they let me know this in no uncertain terms when I made requests for their services in these areas.

At the time, it never occurred to me that some of them were already loaded down with heavy teaching responsibilities or family obligations or both. I suppose I didn't realize that teachers should have lives outside of school. Furthermore, it never crossed my mind that most of the true professional teachers in the school felt that there were better ways to use their time than taking tickets at football games or standing guard in the restrooms during class changes.

Whatever the reasons for rebuffing my invitations to serve, my perceptions about my colleagues' low level of caring frightened and bewildered me for two reasons. In the first place, their attitude toward performing extra duties was totally unexpected on my part. When I agreed to accept the challenge of serving as the principal of the school, I thought that everyone in the school would be as committed as I thought I was to doing everything in their power to serve and support the students, the school, and the community. I suppose this means that I thought the teachers would do exactly what I asked them to do and, furthermore, that they would be pleased as punch for the opportunities that I provided them to show me just how much they cared. I was naive enough to believe that because I was the principal, wherever I looked I would find lots of willing hands and hearts to help me with what I knew would be a formidable task. When the teachers didn't react the way I expected them to, I was taken by surprise.

The second reason I was bewildered and frightened was that I wondered how the school could ever be successful without the combined talents and commitment of all of us in the school working together to realize my vision for the school! I thought all the teachers should get behind me and support my vision for what I believed our school could be. After all, I was the duly appointed leader, and leaders are supposed to have visions for the organizations they lead. Although I hate to admit it, I was afraid that without a high level of commitment on the part of the faculty and staff to my vision for the school, the school might not live up to its promise and I might ultimately fail as a leader.

When I think back on it now, what's incredible to me is that I didn't realize that the only vision that would be at all meaningful to the faculty and staff was not my vision, but rather a shared vision that we all helped to create. Because I lacked this important realization, I didn't do enough to make it appealing or inviting or even possible for my colleagues to demonstrate how much they cared about our students and our school.

As I reflect on it now, I realize that my approach to leadership at that time was very traditional. I tried to lead the school in the ways that I had seen other principals lead. I held the reins of power tightly and sought out others in the school who were comfortable with my approach to leadership and who therefore appeared to me to care as much as I did. I found what I thought were these highly committed individuals and made them my comrades. I gave them more than their fair share of the work and responsibility, but I also gave them more than their fair share of my attention and praise. To be perfectly honest, I suppose that I played "head games" with the teachers to get things done in the way I wanted them done, until one day the teachers decided that they had had enough of my head games, and that was the day they taught me a valuable lesson about sharing power and responsibility.

The school where I was principal was located in a white, middle-class, suburban neighborhood on the outskirts of a fairly large metropolitan area. Almost all the African American students in the school were bused from inner-city neighborhoods located about twelve miles away. Because they lived so far from the school and did not have their own transportation, most of the African American students were not involved in school life beyond taking classes. They rode their buses to school in the mornings and attended their classes; then they got on their buses and returned to their neighborhoods at the end of the school day. Clearly, this was not a healthy situation for the school or the students. The student government association first voiced a concern about the lack of student involvement in school activities and asked that something be done to address the situation. I agreed that something needed to be done to increase the level of involvement of African American students outside the classroom and worked with the administrative team to put a plan in place.

The solution proposed to address the situation was a change in the master schedule that would permit an activities period to be held during the regular school day. By reducing the time allotted to each class on a designated "Activities Friday," enough time could be gleaned from the modified schedule to allow clubs and interest groups to meet and conduct their business during the school day. The arrangement made it possible for all students to be involved in at least one school activity even if they lived a long way from the school or had other commitments such as jobs that kept them from participating in after-school activities.

It was decided that teachers who did not wish to sponsor an activity for students, and students who did not choose to be involved in an activity would be paired during the scheduled activities period in a study hall arrangement. The rest of the teachers and students would meet as scheduled and engage in their selected activities. I don't recall just how these initial decisions were made, although I do remember that the faculty was not directly involved. Beyond that, I don't recall how we made the decisions to structure the program. But regardless of how the decisions were made, we put a plan in place and moved to the implementation stage.

The activities sign-up period was held, and a surprisingly large number of students and teachers opted for the study halls rather than the activities. Undaunted, we forged ahead and scheduled the first Activities Friday of the school year.

The big day arrived. The bell rang. The first activities period commenced. Chaos reigned! While all the teachers and most of the students went to their chosen activities or study halls as scheduled, many did not. Students were everywhere they weren't supposed to be! They were in the parking lot. A fair number went out behind the gymnasium to have a smoke. Some even took the liberty of driving their cars to a nearby strip mall to purchase hamburgers and fries. Being a certifiable control freak, I was more than a little alarmed imagining all the terrible things that might happen to our students while they were supposedly under the school's supervision.

Finally, the activities period ended. We resumed our regular schedule while we counted our losses. Although no one was dead or injured, clearly the experiment had not gone well. I met with the administrative team and we decided that the fundamental problem was not with the activities period per se, but rather with the novelty of the arrangement. After considerable discussion, we came to the unwarranted conclusion that both teachers and students simply needed more time to adjust to the innovation. We reasoned that one time was not enough to make a judgment about whether or not the activities schedule was a good idea, so we reviewed the whole activities day arrangement again in great detail with students and teachers. We made sure this time that all students and teachers knew exactly where they were supposed to be and exactly what they should be doing during the activities period. Then we scheduled our second activities period of the year.

If the first activities period could be termed chaotic, then the second one was chaotic to the power of ten. The second time we held the activities period, a lot of the students who had been in their assigned places the first time around joined their fellow classmates who had opted for the parking lot, the smoking area behind the gymnasium, and the hamburger joints. It had not seemed possible, but the second activities period was even more chaotic than the first—a *lot* more chaotic!

We were understandably discouraged by this unexpected result, but not yet defeated. I called the management team together again, and we reviewed the program in detail. I was determined that we would discover what had gone wrong and devise workable solutions to the problems we were experiencing. Finally, after a lengthy discussion, the administrative team developed three alternative approaches that we thought had a reasonable chance to succeed. For the sake of simplicity, I will call the three approaches Plan A,

Plan B, and Plan C. I told the administrative team that we would share the ideas with the teaching staff at our next faculty meeting and together we would make a decision as to which approach would be selected for implementation. Someone had suggested that perhaps things would work better if the teachers had a hand in making the decision. We all agreed this was a good idea, but even then I knew in my heart that Plan A was the most desirable of the three alternatives, and I was reasonably sure that the teaching staff would cheerfully endorse my preference. At that time, I had no idea that I was in for a few surprises.

The day of the faculty meeting arrived. Right before the meeting was to begin, I received my first surprise. As luck would have it, my boss, the area superintendent of schools, dropped by the school unannounced as I was gathering my materials and preparing to head for the faculty meeting. He decided that he would accompany me to the meeting because he, too, was new in his position and the meeting would provide him with an excellent opportunity to interact with the faculty. The main item on the agenda was the activities period, and although I expected it to generate some discussion, I thought that we would come to a decision—the right decision—in fairly short order.

The meeting began on time, and we proceeded rapidly through the agenda until we reached the item concerning the activities period. I told the group that together we would explore the three proposed alternatives to correct the problems we were experiencing with the activities period. I also let them know that I expected that, after some discussion, we would be able to reach a consensus on the best alternative that we would then implement together. I explained that I preferred to reach consensus on the best approach rather than decide by majority vote, and that we would take all the time necessary to reach consensus. Then I briefed the teachers on each of the three plans and asked for discussion.

As the discussion progressed, it was clear that both Plan A and Plan B had a good deal of support but that nobody much cared for Plan C. In fact, it appeared that the faculty was pretty evenly divided on the first two approaches. So we agreed to eliminate Plan C from further consideration and decide between the two remaining plans. It was at this fatal juncture that I decided that it was time for me to demonstrate my leadership skills. I halted discussion for the moment and reviewed Plans A and B for the group once again. This time, though, as I explained the two plans, I was careful to enhance the advantages associated with Plan A (my preferred plan) while minimizing the disadvantages. Of course, I did the exact reverse when I reviewed Plan B for the group.

We then resumed discussion of the two plans and, to my amazement, not only had the number of supporters for Plan B increased, but they also appeared to be more deeply entrenched in their position than they were before! But I didn't give up. I doggedly continued to champion Plan A, and some of my supporters on the faculty did their best to help me carry the day. But it was a lost cause, and eventually it became evident to everyone in the room that we would never reach consensus.

It was at this point that I finally gave in and told the faculty that it appeared that consensus was impossible, and therefore that we would have to vote on a preferred plan. So we voted, and I suppose I don't have to tell you which plan won a narrow victory. I didn't even try to hide my disappointment as I announced that Plan B had carried the day and that Plan B would be implemented at the next scheduled activities period.

After the meeting had concluded, the area superintendent walked back to my office with me. I think he was pretty amazed by what he had witnessed, but he didn't have too much to say about it. He did, however, have two questions for me. The first was, "Why did you waste all that time?" The second was, "Why didn't you just tell them what you wanted them to do?" To his two questions I had but one answer, and I suspect it sounded about as ridiculous to him at that time as it does to me now. I told him, "I believe in democratic leadership. I think that those who are most affected by decisions should have the right to help make those decisions."

Of course, I wasn't the least bit democratic. I was playing a game with the faculty by trying to manipulate them into believing that they were an integral part of the decision-making process when clearly they were not. And the teachers taught me a lesson by making me look foolish in front of my boss. They made it clear that they had no intention of being manipulated by me. They let me know in a very powerful way that, if I wanted to play games, then they could play games, too. From that day forward, I realized that, if I decided that I needed to give the faculty the opportunity to participate in making an important decision, I had better be prepared for them to make the decision that they wanted to make, and not the one I expected them to make.

We implemented Plan B as the teachers had decided we should and my final surprise was that it worked beautifully. Looking back, that really shouldn't have been a surprise to me. After all, Plan B was the teachers' plan, and they were therefore committed to making it succeed. Immediately after this experience, I made a silent vow that I would never to try to manipulate the faculty again—and I didn't!

Shortly after my activities day lesson in leadership, we established a Faculty Steering Committee in our school that was designed to place teachers at the heart of the decision-making process. The Faculty Steering Committee met monthly and proposed problems that needed to be addressed in the school and offered advice on how to best solve those problems. Believe me when

I tell you that those of us on the administrative team listened carefully to the advice we received from the Faculty Steering Committee!

What did I learn from this experience aside from making the decision to avoid engaging in gamesmanship in the future? I learned that it is not the leader's prerogative, or even his or her responsibility, to make all the important decisions in the school. If we are ever to see teachers and principals effectively leading together, then there must be some substantial changes made in the ways we think and feel about our personal and shared leadership responsibilities in the school.

I learned that if you are the formal leader, you have to give others in the organization both a reason and the opportunity to demonstrate that they care by finding ways to involve them in meaningful decision making. People naturally care a great deal more about the decisions they make than the decisions that are made for them by others. But perhaps the most important thing that I learned from my Friday Activities debacle was that *a school isn't going anywhere that the people who make up the school—students, staff, and faculty— don't want it to go.*

I am grateful for all these lessons. They have served me well over the years. How about you? Are you willing to share power and responsibility with others in your organization? Is caring presently demonstrated in the ways in which decisions get made in your organization? If not, then what can you do about it? What are you willing to do to effectively share power and responsibility with others?

TAKE TIME TO REFLECT

1. Describe a time when you thought you had "the right answer" to a particular problem only to discover that it wasn't the right answer at all. Did you doggedly hold on to your notion of the right answer against mounting evidence that it may not be right at all? What was the result? Do you think that there could have been a better result if you had been more open to the ideas of others in this particular situation? If you had it to do over again, what would you do differently? Share your stories with others if you are working with a group.

2. Think about several key decisions that have resulted in a significant change in your school or organization over the past year or two. Select one of these key decisions and trace the decision-making process from the origination of the idea for a change, through the development of a plan to accomplish the change, to the implementation of the plan. What individual or group suggested that a change be made? Who was involved in the decision to actually make the change, and how was that decision made? Who were the major participants in planning for the change and what was their level of involvement? How successfully was the change implemented? Could implementation of the change have been more successful through wider participation or meaningful involvement by others in the decision-making process? How?

CHAPTER TEN

WHAT DOES IT MEAN TO BE RESPONSIBLE?

There is an old story about an ambitious young school administrator, Robert, who received a telephone call out of the blue from the local school superintendent late one afternoon in early August. The superintendent told Robert that he had some bad news and some good news for him. The bad news was that, after a great deal of thought and discussion with the school board, the superintendent had made a decision to fire the current principal of the local high school, George, who had been on the job for many years. The good news was that the superintendent had selected Robert to be the replacement for the veteran principal and the board had enthusiastically endorsed his decision. The superintendent congratulated Robert on his selection to this important leadership role and advised him to immediately get over to the school and relieve his predecessor who had already been informed of his firing.

Robert's head was spinning and he was torn by conflicting emotions as he drove to the high school to carry out the superintendent's directive. He liked George and was genuinely sorry to see his tenure as principal end in this way. On the other hand, being appointed principal at such a tender age was a great boost to Robert's career and boded well for the young man's future with the district. Robert couldn't wait to tell his wife, Linda, who would be so proud of him. And just wait until his friends found out; they would be so envious when they realized that Robert was progressing much more quickly in his career than they were. And he would probably get a substantial pay raise, his own secretary, and the parking place right by the front door with the sign that proclaimed "Reserved for Principal." Although he regretted George's misfortune, Robert felt a growing sense of excitement and exhilaration at this unexpected opportunity that had fallen into his lap.

Robert's step quickened as he strode along the hallway to the principal's office, and then it slowed as he thought about facing George. Robert couldn't help but wonder about the reception he would receive from the outgoing principal. Clearly, George could not be pleased that his tenure had come to such an abrupt and unceremonious conclusion. But then again, what did Robert have to do with George's firing anyway? Absolutely nothing! So the newly appointed principal simply gritted his teeth and moved ahead with determination, fully expecting that he would not receive a very warm welcome from the man he was succeeding.

But when he finally arrived at the principal's office, Robert was stunned by how graciously he was received by the man he was replacing. In fact, George seemed totally unaffected by his personal misfortune. He even appeared to be somewhat jovial in his demeanor. He smiled at his replacement's obvious discomfort and told him not to be concerned in the least. George explained that he had known for some time that his days were numbered and that he was frankly relieved that the ax had finally fallen and he could get on with his life and his career. The old veteran shook Robert's hand warmly as he told the younger man that if he had to be replaced, he was truly gratified that his replacement would be someone whom he admired and respected. To prove his point, George told Robert that he was going to give him something that would help him as he made the transition to the role of principal.

With that, he placed two sealed envelopes, marked #1 and #2, in the new principal's hand as he said, "Take these two envelopes and put them in a very safe place. Based on my experience, I can assure you that a time will come when you will face a difficult crisis here at the school that you won't be able to resolve no matter how hard you try. When that time comes, take out the first envelope and read it. I can just about promise you that the words I have written will help you to successfully extricate yourself from the crisis that you are facing." George sternly cautioned Robert not to use the envelopes carelessly, but to use them only after he had first exhausted every other possibility. George again warmly shook his successor's hand, handed him the keys to the building, climbed into his car, and drove away.

Robert placed the two envelopes in the top drawer of his desk and soon forgot all about them. For a time, things went extremely well for him and the school. The faculty and staff had grown weary of the old leadership and they embraced Robert in his new role. They genuinely liked the new man, and everyone went out of the way to help Robert succeed. As a result, the new principal enjoyed an extended honeymoon that stretched over the better part of a year. The school ran smoothly and Robert received high praise from the superintendent. Life was good!

Then suddenly, and without warning, it happened. A seemingly routine problem presented itself. Robert applied what he thought was the proper solution, but the problem persisted. Day by day, the situation grew more ominous. The young principal tried another solution, but that one, too, proved ineffective, and the problem only increased in size and intensity. With a growing sense of alarm, Robert tried a third solution and was terrified when the problem spun out of control and substantially disrupted the entire school and even spilled over into the community.

Suddenly, it seemed as if Robert's friends and supporters had become invisible. Colleagues and constituents who had formerly praised his leadership skills were now silent on the subject; some were even openly critical. Meanwhile, the faculty and staff grew more restless and impatient for a solution to the crisis. The young principal became more and more desperate with each passing day.

Night and day, he racked his brain for a way out of the crisis. Just when all seemed lost, he remembered the envelopes that had been given to him by the man he had succeeded. He raced to his office, jerked open the top drawer of his desk, and felt around for the two envelopes. At last he found them, ripped open the one marked #1 and eagerly read what was written. The message, written in George's large, plain scrawl proclaimed, "Blame it on me!" Robert was dumbstruck. "Blame it on me!" he muttered. Then a light came on in his head, and he understood.

Robert immediately called a general staff meeting and explained that the crisis the school was facing was not of his own doing. He told all those present that the dire situation they were facing was the direct result of some poor decisions that had been made by his predecessor and that he, Robert, because of his lack of involvement in making those poor decisions, was blameless. He asked that everyone rally behind his leadership and assured them that together they would solve the problems they were facing. The people listened, and a sense of relief washed over Robert as he saw some of them begin to nod their heads in agreement. Soon, they were all nodding and agreeing that the old principal, George, was indeed the responsible party. The faculty and staff rallied behind Robert, things got better, and thanks to the sage advice in that first envelope, a potential disaster had been averted. The young school leader breathed a deep sigh of relief, thanked his lucky stars, and paid sincere tribute in his heart to his wise predecessor.

Life in the school returned to normal. For quite some time, everything ran like clockwork and Robert relaxed and grew more comfortable and confident in his leadership role. But alas! One day another crisis appeared on the horizon. Like the initial crisis, it grew and grew, despite the actions the young principal took to resolve the situation. After much reflection and a fair amount of gnashing of teeth, Robert remembered that he still had that second envelope that he had not yet used. "Thank goodness!" he exclaimed as he raced to his office to retrieve his salvation from the top desk drawer. He searched frantically for the magic envelope, grasped it in his sweaty hands, and gleefully ripped it open. The simple message, again written in George's own hand read, "Prepare two envelopes!"

The central point to this little story is unmistakable: When all is said and done, the leader is the person who retains the ultimate responsibility for success or failure in an organizational setting. He or she cannot pass that responsibility along to someone else in times of crisis. Some leaders may get by for a time on their good looks, personalities, or political connections. Some can even survive for awhile by blaming others for their own shortcomings. But at some point, a day of reckoning is bound to come for any leader, and that leader's mettle will be tested. These are the "defining moments" that Badaracco (1997) has referred to as "crucibles of characters" that shape leaders and their organizations.

During my first year as a high school principal, I received a lot of lessons in responsibility. One that stands out took place during the fall of that first year. In South Carolina, school personnel were required to fill out annual basic educational data survey (BEDS) reports. These reports were designed to help the South Carolina Department of Education monitor personnel and programs throughout the state by systematically collecting information related to teachers' areas of certification and teaching assignments, as well as other information critical to providing all students with a defined minimum educational program. A portion of the BEDS report was especially designed to be answered by the principal of a school. This section of the report, which was referred to as "the list of assurances," presented fifty general statements related to school program standards, to which the principal was required to respond with a simple "yes" or "no," depending on whether or not the principal judged the standard to be met or not met. It was sort of an honor system of school accountability. The fifty items ran the gamut from health-room facilities, to playground areas, to instructional leadership. In fact, the first item at the top of the list of assurances pertained to the principal's responsibility to provide instructional leadership and was stated something like this: "The principal spends 50 percent of his or her time in instructional leadership." As it turned out, completing that list of assurances for the first time created quite a dilemma for me.

I recall sitting at my desk, sharpened No. 2 pencil in hand, ready to discharge my responsibilities by completing the principal's portion of the BEDS report. I was stumped, however, by that first item on instructional leadership. Although I was reasonably certain that the expected response to the item, "The principal spends 50 percent of his or her time on instructional leadership," was "yes," I was even more certain that the more truthful response was "no." Technically, the correct response wasn't even included in either of the two choices that had been provided for me. The correct response would have been something like, "You've got to be kidding!" or "You have definitely lost your mind if you think principals can spend 50 percent of their time in instructional leadership!"

One of the advantages of being a rookie principal in a large school district is that there is always someone older and wiser to answer questions for you. The person I chose to answer this particular question for me was the secondary supervisor in the district office. He had been a successful principal in the district for a number of years prior to earning his district office assignment, and I felt comfortable sharing my dilemma with him. So, I called Don on the telephone, and the conversation went something like this:

Me: Don, I'm having a problem completing the assurances section of the BEDS report.

Don: What's your problem?

Me: I don't know how to answer the first item. It says that the principal spends 50 percent of his or her time in instructional leadership.

Don: Mark it "yes."

Me: Don, I know I'm probably expected to mark the item "yes," but truthfully, I don't spend 50 percent of my time in instructional leadership. I'll bet I don't even spend 10 percent of my time in instructional leadership.

Don: Hell! Mark it "yes"! Everybody marks it "yes"!

I politely thanked Don for his assistance, hung up the telephone, and marked the question "no." After all, I was a brand-new principal—I still had my integrity! And just to demonstrate how much integrity I had, I marked six or seven other items "no" as well. I completed my report, bundled it up with the teachers' finished reports, and sent the whole thing off to my assigned supervisor in the department of education. I thought that would be the end of it. I had done my duty while preserving my integrity. I had answered each of the items as honestly as I could, and I was feeling pretty good about myself.

Sometime around the end of November that year, I received an unexpected response to my BEDS report from my supervisor in the department of education. For each of the items to which I had responded "no," he had two more questions for me to answer. The first question was, "Why not?" The second question was, "What do you plan to do about it?" As an added bonus for the honesty I had displayed, I received a letter of reprimand from my district superintendent for making the school district look bad!

The answer to the first question, "Why not?" was complex. There were a lot of reasons why not. I was a new principal struggling hard just to survive in an alien environment. I didn't know how to be an instructional leader. Somehow, they'd forgotten to teach me how to be an instructional leader in graduate school, and I hadn't been given the opportunity to learn those skills during my two years as an assistant principal in a different school in the district. To complicate matters further, the learning curve was huge for me as a first-year principal, and I was spending inordinate amounts of time on routine tasks that would have been better left to others. As noted earlier, I was a control freak and hadn't yet learned how to delegate effectively. There were a lot of other reasons I could have come up with to justify why not, but I think you get the point.

As for my state supervisor's second question, "What do you plan to do about it?" that particular question was far easier for me to answer than the "Why not?" question. From that day forward I planned to check "yes" on all the assurances!

Once I had recovered from the shock of being taken to task, I was able to think more about the two questions my state supervisor had posed for me. On reflection, I was forced to admit to myself that they were reasonable questions and that I was the one who had the responsibility to answer them in a satisfactory manner. If I wasn't spending 50 percent of my time in instructional leadership, and that was the expectation for the principal of a school, then I damn well better find a way to do it. If my health room was inadequate or my playgrounds unsuitable, then it was my job to see that these situations were remedied. It wasn't enough for me smugly to check "no" on an annual survey from the department of education. It was my responsibility to work within the system to do whatever was required to make the correct answer "yes"!

Experienced leaders are all well aware that that there are good things and not-so-good things that go with hand in hand with the responsibilities of leadership. In their revealing book, *Leadership on the Line*, Heifetz and Linsky (2002) do a wonderful job of describing some of the rewards and costs associated with the responsibilities of leadership. While they are quick to recognize the privilege and joys of leadership, they are also honest in acknowledging the difficulties and sacrifice involved in being responsible for the welfare of an organization:

Each day brings you opportunities to raise important questions, speak to higher values, and surface unresolved conflicts. Every day you have the chance to make a difference in the lives of people around you. (p. 2)

We [those who would be leaders] like the feeling of stepping up to the plate and having the crowds cheer us on. Yet raising questions that go to the core of people's habits goes unrewarded, at least for awhile. You get booed instead of cheered. In fact, it may be a long time before you hear any applause—if ever. They may throw tomatoes. They may shoot bullets. Leadership takes the capacity to stomach hostility so that you can stay connected to people lest you disengage them and exacerbate the danger. (p. 18)

Heifetz and Linsky (2002) caution would-be leaders that "learning to take the heat and receive people's anger in a way that does not undermine your initiative is one of the toughest tasks of leadership" (p. 140). They also remind us of the human costs of leadership: "For people who find taking casualties extremely painful, almost too painful to endure, this part of leadership presents a special dilemma. But it often goes with the territory" (p. 99).

So what does responsibility in a leadership role mean to you? Do you willingly embrace the ultimate responsibility that accompanies the mantle of leader? Are you comfortable with accepting responsibility—not just for your own actions, but also for the actions of those whom you lead? Can you reject the temptation to blame others for poor decisions that lead to poor results? Are you willing to share the credit for successes, but shoulder the ultimate blame for failures? Can you take the heat that is the frequent traveling companion of difficult decisions? Finally, do you care enough about the mission and goals of the organization to be willing to endure the extreme pain that comes with taking casualties?

TAKE TIME TO REFLECT

1. Suppose that for some reason you are suddenly forced to leave your present position, and you genuinely want to do your successor a favor by leaving two pieces of advice in separate envelopes that would help him or her lead successfully. Based on your knowledge and experience, what advice would you provide in each of your two envelopes? If you are working in a group, share your advice with the others in the group.

2. As accountability issues have assumed a more central place in the operation of schools, school leaders have seen the need to increasingly share power and responsibility with a host of other major stakeholders in the school community. Who are some of these major stakeholders, and what would you suggest are ways that school leaders can continue to function and be perceived as strong leaders while dealing effectively with issues of accountability?

CHAPTER ELEVEN

WHY AM I DOING THIS?

I f the question, "What do I care about?" is the single most critical question that school leaders can ask themselves, then the question, "Why am I doing this?" might be a close second. Leaders make dozens and dozens of decisions every day. They are constantly struggling with what they should do in certain situations and how they should do it. Because of the sheer numbers of decisions that leaders must make and the limited time they have available in which to make them, it's easy—and even convenient—for leaders to forget why they are choosing one course of action over another and what the effects of their decisions might be on all the constituent groups and individuals they serve.

Despite the many decisions to be made and the crush of limited time available in which to make them, leaders need to realize that behind every decision is a motive or a reason that drives that decision. It's probably more accurate if we acknowledge that there are, in fact, numerous motives driving the decisions that we make as leaders. These motives are varied in intensity and purpose and so intermingled that it is extremely difficult to even acknowledge them, must less to decipher and understand them.

If we are completely honest with ourselves, we would all be forced to admit that while most of our motives underlying the decisions that we make are decent and noble, others may not be so decent and noble. Sometimes, we make a particular decision because we care about others and truly want to help someone in need. Other times, we may take a course of action not because it will necessarily help someone in need, but because we are expected to take that action in a given situation. For example, we may recommend a student for expulsion for bringing alcohol on to the school campus. Although we may genuinely feel that expulsion may not be the best decision for this particular student, we are expected to enforce the district's policies, and those policies dictate the required decision. At other times, we make certain decisions because it is our job to do so. We develop a master schedule and give teachers their teaching assignments, arrange duty rosters, and so forth because these routine tasks have to be done and it is our job to make the necessary decisions to see that these tasks are accomplished.

A number of other motives for our decisions are not nearly as laudable as those I have mentioned thus far. In addition to wanting to help others or to meet the expectations of others or to carry out our job responsibilities, there are any number of not-so-nice motives for the decisions that leaders make. For example, sometimes we make decisions to assert our authority as leaders. We take a particular course of action simply because we can! By making a particular decision, we can feel superior, powerful, and in control of the situation. Sometimes, by choosing a specific course of action we can put certain people in their places and reaffirm the pecking order. Other times, we may use decisions to punish people, to teach them a lesson, or to get even for some real or imagined transgression. At still other times, we may make a decision because we know that by doing so we can put someone in our debt, or perhaps we will decide an issue in a way that repays someone else to whom we feel indebted.

All these nice and not-so-nice motives are lurking in the shadows, ready to creep into the decisions of leaders who are not vigilant enough to ask themselves the critical question, "Why am I doing this?" As Greenleaf (1996) notes, "A capable supervisor is necessarily a student of motives, not necessarily versed in the jargon of the professionals but nevertheless is ever watchful of the effect of each order, suggestion, or word of advice on each individual" (p. 180).

In my role as a high school principal, I always thought of myself as being extremely student oriented. I felt it was my sacred duty to be a powerful and outspoken advocate for the young people in our school and to use my position and the authority that went with it in every way possible to see that the interests of children were promoted and protected. As might be expected, I had lots of opportunities to test my resolve in my efforts to be an effective advocate for children. One of those opportunities came to me one afternoon in the late spring when the parents of one of the students in our school came to my office to meet with me about a problem their son was facing.

Although I had never met either Mr. or Mrs. Curry, I did know their son, Richard, who was a member of the senior class. I could tell instantly that the Currys were upset, and it didn't take them long to explain why. They told me that Richard was experiencing a personal crisis and they had reached the end of their rope in their efforts to help him deal with it.

Mr. Curry briefly recounted for me Richard's sterling record as a high school student. He told me that Richard had never made a grade lower than a B in his entire school career and had been tapped into the National Honor Society when he was just a sophomore. Because of his success on the PSAT, Richard had been named a Merit Scholar semifinalist the previous fall. In addition to his academic prowess, Richard had been actively involved in student life, and had been a member of student government for several years in addition to serving as the coeditor of the yearbook during his junior year. As the result of his outstanding academic achievement coupled with his record of student leadership, Richard's family had recently been notified that he was a finalist for a prestigious scholarship at an Ivy League college. But the Currys were terrified that all the success their son had achieved was about to evaporate right before their eyes.

Mrs. Curry told me that her son's behavior had recently become erratic. Richard, who had always been outgoing and friendly, had suddenly become sullen and moody. He had begun to display frequent fits of anger, during which he smashed objects in his room and cried uncontrollably. Richard's old friends had stopped coming around to the house, and his parents suspected that his new friends were into drugs. In their desperation to help their son, the Currys had consulted a psychiatrist, who confirmed their own feelings that Richard was suffering from depression. Although Richard was being treated for depression and his parents were beginning to see some positive results of the treatment, there was a pressing problem that they needed my help in resolving.

Several weeks before my meeting with the Currys, their son had skipped school on the day that an important physics examination was given. Because Richard had received an unexcused absence for that day, the physics teacher had refused to allow Richard to make up his examination and had instead given him a grade of zero. The zero dropped Richard's grade in physics from an A– to a D for the semester. Mr. Curry explained to me that the D in physics was a much more serious problem than might ordinarily be the case because it would probably disqualify Richard from further consideration for his pending scholarship at the Ivy League college and negate all the years of hard work that he had put in to get himself to this point in his academic career. To complicate the situation further, the psychiatrist had warned the Currys that, in his professional judgment, their son might be suicidal, and he advised them that it was critical that Richard not be subjected to any undue stress or pressure at this particular time in his life. With that explanation, the Currys asked me to please intercede with the teacher on behalf of their son and see that he received an opportunity to make up the examination.

I was deeply touched by the Currys' story. I told them not to worry. I promised that I would talk with the teacher as soon as I possibly could, and I assured these deeply troubled parents that the teacher, Mr. Kidd, would provide their son with an opportunity to make up the missed examination and redeem his grade. Little did I know that I was in for the shock of my professional life when I approached Mr. Kidd on behalf of Richard Curry!

When I promised Mr. and Mrs. Curry that I would intercede on behalf of their son, I assumed that there was only one proper course of action to take in this situation, and that was to allow Richard to make up the examination. Clearly, this decision was in the student's best interest, and I felt it was my responsibility to see that the school acted in his interest. Furthermore, I assumed that Mr. Kidd would clearly see it that way and that once I explained the situation to him the matter would be quickly and neatly resolved. However, when I made what I thought was a reasonable request to Mr. Kidd that Richard be allowed to make up the examination and perhaps be penalized a letter grade or so for his failure to take it at the scheduled time, I was met with a polite but stern refusal. Mr. Kidd reminded me that the rules did not allow students to make up work for days on which they received unexcused absences and that he was going to enforce the rules come hell or high water!

When Mr. Kidd responded to me in this unexpected way, I realized that I would have to share some of the important details of this particular situation so that he could understand that this situation was indeed unique and justified breaking (or at least bending) the rules. But I didn't tell him that Richard might be suicidal, because the parents had asked me not to reveal this particular detail unless it was absolutely unavoidable. Instead, I shared some of the other important details of the situation with Mr. Kidd, such as Richard's sterling record and potential scholarship.

The physics teacher remained intractable in his position, however. He assured me that he had no intention of bowing to parental pressure and violating his principles when it came to assigning grades to his students, no matter what the circumstances. At that point, I knew that I had to play my ace card. I told Mr. Kidd about the mental state of his student, and I shared my feelings that perhaps Richard would do something foolish if he were not allowed to make up the examination.

I was astonished when Mr. Kidd was unmoved by my argument. He told me, "Look, stop bothering me about this! I've already told you that I'm not going to allow Richard to make up the examination!" With that declaration, I made the transition from frustration with the situation to anger with the teacher. Driven by my anger, I moved swiftly into my power mode. "Mr. Kidd, I'm not asking you any longer," I said. "I'm telling you! You will arrange for Richard to make up the examination!"

Richard made up the examination, although I don't recall whether or not he received his scholarship. But I do know that he graduated and went off to college somewhere, and I'm fairly certain that he didn't take his own life, because I would have read about it in the newspaper. In addition to all these consequences of my decision to allow Richard to make up his physics exam, there was one additional important consequence. I destroyed the professional relationship that I had previously enjoyed with the physics teacher. Because of this one disagreement and the way in which I handled it, I was never again able to earn back his respect or win his support.

I've told myself many times over the years that I made the right decision. After all, the student was given an opportunity to correct a mistake he had made, and he didn't take drastic action to end his life. I have consoled myself for the loss of the physics teacher's support with the question "What else could I have done in a situation like this where the stakes appeared to be impossibly high?"

But when I am really honest with myself, I am forced to ask myself the question, "Why did I do this?" That's when I see a different side to the situation. When I started out to resolve the problem, my motives were unquestionably pure. I was genuinely concerned for Richard's welfare. I wanted to help him, and I wanted to help set his troubled parents' minds at ease.

But as the situation evolved, my pure motives got tangled up with some not-so-pure motives. When the teacher resisted my attempts to resolve the problem in the way I thought it should be resolved, I began to feel that my authority was being challenged and that my leadership and my professional judgment were being called into question. At some point in our exchange, my motives shifted from genuinely wanting to help Richard and his parents to wanting to put this defiant teacher in his place, to show him who was boss, and to reaffirm my power as the leader in the school. When I'm being completely honest with myself, I also admit that I wasn't about to let a teacher show me up in the community. In my heart of hearts, I had no intention of having Richard's parents telling all their friends and neighbors that I didn't keep my word to them and that I allowed a teacher to walk all over me and their son.

Although I still feel that it was the correct decision to allow Richard to make up his examination, I hope that I could arrive at that decision in a different manner if confronted with a similar situation today. If I could do it over, I would involve the teacher from the beginning and earnestly seek his or her advice and counsel. I now realize that I usurped the teacher's authority and called his professionalism into question by excluding him from the decision-making process. It is little wonder he resisted me as strongly as he did. If I were a principal today, I would make sure that I had a mechanism such as an appeals committee, composed of teachers and other staff members, for deciding when to make exceptions to established policy. Most of all, I would ask myself, "Why am I doing this?" so that I could avoid taking significant actions for the wrong reasons.

The most important lesson here is for school leaders to realize that there are motives for just about every action taken. These motives vary in intensity and purpose and can shift dramatically at a moment's notice. Some of these motives are extremely positive, whereas others are equally negative. If we are truly committed to fulfilling our responsibilities to those we lead, it is imperative that we take the time to examine the motives behind our actions and that we do so in a timely manner.

Examining one's motives is vital to effective leadership: humans are closely attuned to the motives that underlie the actions of others. Most people seem to be able to sense intuitively whether those in leadership roles are doing what they are doing for the right or the wrong reasons. If others in the organization perceive the motives underlying the leaders' decisions as being essentially positive, they will support these leaders in their decisions and assist them in their efforts to lead. They will continue to stand behind these leaders, even when the decisions turn out poorly, because they believe the decisions were made for the right reasons. On the other hand, if others in the organization judge the motives underlying a leader's decisions to be negative, then they will resist those decisions and challenge the authority of the leader at every opportunity. In these instances, poor decisions by leaders will be judged harshly and leaders will be left alone to face the consequences of those poor decisions.

Leaders must strive to become reflective in the sense that they think about and closely study both their thoughts and deeds related to providing leadership for others. They need to dissect their actions by constantly asking questions such as the following:

1. What was the nature of the problem that I was attempting to solve?

2. What actions did I take?

3. What were the positive and negative consequences of those actions?

4. What would I do differently if I had to do it again?

5. Can I in some way make up for the mistakes that I have made and the harm that I may have caused to others?

Most important, leaders need to ask themselves that critical question, "Why am I doing this?" on a regular and routine basis. If you as a leader ask yourself this question and you don't like the answer you give yourself, then you almost certainly need to change your behavior or at least reexamine your values or rearrange your priorities. On the other hand, if you find that you are gratified by the answer you receive, then chances are that others will be gratified as well, and they will demonstrate their gratification by trusting you enough to allow you to lead. In the words of Mark Twain, leaders should "always do right—this will gratify some people and astonish the rest."

TAKE TIME TO REFLECT

1. Try to recall a decision you made recently while acting in some kind of leadership role (e.g., formal work role, parenting role, informal group leader). Why did you make that particular decision? Were there both positive and negative motives underlying the decision? What were some of these motives? What were the positive and negative consequences of your decision? If you had to make the same decision again, what, if anything, would you change?

2. Make a commitment to keep a diary for two weeks. For each day during this period, take a few minutes to recall two or three work-related decisions that you made during that particular day. Honestly evaluate each decision by listing the motives, both positive and negative, that drove that decision. Ask yourself why you made each decision that you made and try to determine if your motives were consistent with who you want to be as a leader. In the event that you don't like some of the motives that drove your decisions, make a commitment to do your best to control the power of these negative motives in the decisions you will make in the days that follow. At the end of the period, critique your progress in monitoring and controlling your motives for deciding issues.

CHAPTER TWELVE

AM I WILLING TO JUMP FOR THE TRAPEZE?

For the last several years that I served on the faculty at the University of South Carolina, I taught a leadership institute each spring with two of my female colleagues. My colleagues had started the institute five or six years earlier and had restricted enrollment to women because they knew that women leaders face a number of unique obstacles that need special attention. By designing an institute especially for women, they reasoned that they would be able to confront these obstacles head-on without the distraction of always having to justify their content and methodology to a group of males who had absolutely no idea where they were coming from.

Their plan worked well—so well, in fact, that they eventually decided that it was time to bring men into the conversation and see if men and women could talk to each other about what it means to lead from both the male and the female perspectives. So the institute was opened to men for the first time, and I was given the opportunity to team-teach the institute with my two colleagues.

The leadership institute was conceived as a continuously evolving exercise with the frequent addition of new ideas and activities. The first couple of years, the institute included a set of exercises that is commonly known as a "ropes course." The ropes course is a set of team-building activities that drive home the importance of communication and cooperation to the accomplishment of group and individual goals. The first year that we used the ropes course, which was shortly after it included men, we included only the low-ropes exercises because we didn't know how many of our students would be willing to participate in the high ropes. The low-ropes exercises, although challenging in many respects, allow participants to keep one foot on the ground at all times. The high-ropes exercises, on the other hand, include some challenging activities that take place high above the ground. Finally, we decided that we should give participants an opportunity to stretch themselves a bit if they were so inclined, and we added the option of participating in some exercises on the high ropes.

At this point, I should mention that I do not enjoy being in high places. I make it a habit to always keep at least one foot firmly planted on terra firma. In fact, I would like traveling by plane a whole lot better if they taxied from one city to the next rather than actually becoming airborne. So, as you can probably guess, including the high-ropes exercises in the institute was certainly not my idea!

The students in the institute had the option of participating in one of two exercises on the high ropes. One of these exercises produced some unexpected and even wonderful results. It required the participant to climb a telephone pole by grasping small rings attached to either side of the pole. When participants in this particular exercise arrived near the top of the pole, which was about thirty or so feet off the ground, they had to pull themselves up until they were able to stand with both feet on top of the pole. If you think this sounds difficult and scary, you should try standing on the ground and looking up at someone standing on the top of the pole. It *is* difficult and it is definitely scary!

This exercise is not the least bit dangerous. It just feels dangerous— really dangerous! The participant is protected from falling during the exercise by a harness fastened around the waist and secured to a rope-and-pulley security system that is capably manned by a team of fellow participants on the ground.

Once a participant has successfully climbed the telephone pole and is standing with both feet firmly planted on top, the next challenge is to jump off the pole and attempt to grasp a trapeze suspended at eye level approximately six to eight feet from the pole. If the participant successfully grasps the trapeze, the exercise is completed and the triumphant (trust me, this is the right word) warrior is then lowered slowly to the ground by the pulley, to be greeted by the love and adoration of her or his fellow participants. If the participant jumps and fails to grasp the trapeze, then, after a sudden jolt resulting from a falling human body being jerked to a halt by the rope attached to the harness, the participant is slowly lowered to the ground, also to be greeted by the love and adoration of his or her fellow participants.

The glorious reception one receives on the ground is not reserved for participants who are successful in grasping the trapeze. The reception is given to all those who successfully conquer their fears enough to climb all the way to the top of the pole and make the leap. The participants, those who have already jumped or those who are waiting to jump, understand that the real accomplishment is not in grasping the trapeze: it is in trusting yourself and your colleagues enough to jump for it. If truth be told, it is probably an even greater accomplishment to jump and miss the trapeze than it is to jump and grasp it successfully.

We were amazed that first time as we watched students perform on the high ropes. There were some we were certain would absolutely relish the opportunity to show all the others participants just what they were capable of doing and they didn't disappoint us. We were overwhelmed, however, by others who surprised us by not only accepting the challenge, but also—at the same time—conquering their fears.

The classic example was a young Korean woman who hadn't been in the country long enough to build close friendships. As she climbed the pole, she was obviously terrified. Her hands shook, and her voice faltered when she attempted to speak. When she neared the top on her climb up the pole, she hesitated a long time before she was finally able, with the encouragement of her fellow participants, to pull herself all the way up until she was standing with both feet on the summit. Looking up from thirty feet away, we could all clearly see that fear gripped the heart of the small figure balancing precariously on the summit of the pole. Several times, she started to climb down without attempting to jump for the trapeze, but her colleagues on the ground wouldn't permit her to stop short of her goal. They called up words of encouragement to her; they assured her that she could do it and that they were there to catch her if she should miss.

After what seemed like an eternity, she gave in to the overwhelming wave of support that was radiating up from the ground. She jumped into space and missed the trapeze, only to be caught by the safety harness. A roar of approval went up from the ground below. As she was safely lowered to the ground by the rope attached to the safety harness, she received more love and adoration from the group than anyone else who attempted the exercise during the entire day. I am convinced that this happened because everyone realized just how much more courage it required for her to perform the exercise than had been required from any of the others who attempted the feat that day.

Leadership feels a lot like standing on top of that pole and looking out into space. In fact, the practice of leadership is much like a series of ropes courses, all with varying degrees of difficulty. The leader is constantly confronted with new challenges. In every situation, he or she must weigh the potential to realize gain against the potential to experience loss and, even, at times, total disaster. The need to feel safe is very powerful, but the rewards that come with personal, professional, and organizational growth are equally alluring. Only the person standing on the top of the pole—the leader—can decide whether the anxiety produced by the fear of falling is such a powerful deterrent that it prohibits one from even trying—or if the excitement of the jump, the exhilaration of soaring like a bird through the air, is satisfying enough to encourage one to do it again and again. Whether or not a leader-chooses to jump off the top of the telephone pole is dependent not only on weighing the balance of the potential risks versus the rewards, but also on the kind of organization around the leader that he or she has developed.

Some leaders build organizations where risk is avoided at all cost. The chief goal of such organizations invariably becomes safety rather than growth. Not only does the leader avoid risks, but he or she discourages others in the organization from taking the unnecessary chances that always accompany trying new and difficult things. Over time, these organizations become stagnant; they lose their edge and become boring and unrewarding places to work.

Other leaders build organizations where risk taking is encouraged and effort is celebrated and rewarded just as much as success. Such leaders are never out on the high wire alone. They build a safety net of mutual trust and respect that can sustain them should they fall. These risk-taking leaders are the best leaders because the organizations they lead are dynamic and vital; they encourage human beings to test their limits to the maximum and to taste the sweet nectar of success. As Kouzes and Posner (1995) note, "Wise leaders recognize failure as a necessary fact of the innovative life. Instead of punishing it, they encourage it; instead of trying to fix blame for mistakes, they learn from them; instead of adding rules, they encourage flexibility" (p. 79).

A number of years ago, I was a member of a team of researchers that conducted a national study of high school principals and their schools. One of the findings that emerged from our study was a clear relationship between risk-taking behavior and school success. We discovered that when principals, teachers, and other staff members had healthy appetites for risk, they were more likely to experience positive growth. In fact, we became convinced that the more risks, the bigger the risks, and the more people involved in risk-taking behavior, the better the results.

An appetite for risk in an organizational setting may be especially important because most organizations, especially public schools and school districts, tend to be highly bureaucratic in nature. Many top-level leaders fear the uncertainties of dealing with the unknown and, therefore, tend to be inflexible and resistant to change. In this kind of environment, it is no wonder that calculated risk-taking behavior on the part of a leader can lend an air of excitement and energy to organizations that helps relieve the institutional boredom that saps the vitality of the workforce day after day, week after week, month after month, and year after year.

Why are some leaders willing to take risks while others choose to play it safe? The best leaders take risks not because they are foolhardy or careless, but because they realize the effect that risk-taking behavior has on others. Risk-taking leaders are not loose cannons on deck. On the contrary, they are thoughtful planners who realize that a failure today doesn't preclude success in the future but that a failure to try will surely preclude success in the present as well as the future. Kouzes and Posner (1995) have described the effect of risk-taking behavior on people and organizations:

> People are inspired by those who take initiative and who risk personal safety for the sake of a cause. Only those who act boldly in times of crisis and change are going to succeed. Without courage there can be no hope—and little chance of survival in today's highly volatile economic and social situations. (p. 77)

Anyone who wishes to lead must realize that any worthwhile pursuit involves a significant element of risk. A successful business leader might take a gamble on a new product line; a world-class ice skater in the heat of competition might disdain a simpler maneuver and go for the risky quadruple jump, risking everything for the chance to win it all. Think about it. Did you ever see a figure skater win an Olympic gold medal by doing a simple routine perfectly? I don't believe that I ever have or that I ever will.

I absolutely believe that the most successful role models in any endeavor are those willing to risk a temporary failure for the opportunity to experience long-term success. In a spine-tingling scene from the popular movie *Top Gun* (Simpson, Bruckheimer, & Scott, 1993), the brash young aviator played by Tom Cruise flies his Tomcat jet fighter upside down mere inches from a Russian MiG. Behavior like that is a far cry from the standard operating procedures outlined for naval pilots, but it shows the mettle of those considered to be the best of the best—the so-called top guns!

Like championship figure skaters and top gun fighter pilots, school leaders—at least the extraordinary ones—knowingly and willingly assume risks. A teacher who is willing to look foolish by running around the classroom flapping her arms to dramatize the flight of Icarus is so much more exciting, inspiring, and wonderful than one who simply describes Icarus with words. I've witnessed one of the finest teachers in the school where I served as principal in just such a display. By the way, she was one of those very special teacher leaders who cared tremendously about the school and the students and showed that caring in countless ways. Believe me: The students loved her for her willingness to make herself vulnerable! I loved her for it too, and wished that I could find a way to encourage all the teachers in our school to run around and flap their arms on a more regular basis.

Risk-taking leaders understand that taking risks is part and parcel of soaring with the eagles. They also realize that by taking risks, they are making themselves vulnerable to the criticism and second-guessing of others with less stout hearts. They are, however, more than willing to subject themselves to second-guessing because they know that by making themselves vulnerable, they encourage others in their organizations to do the same. They understand that if, as leaders, they take risks in pursuit of the goals of the organization, then others will be much more inclined to take risks, too. I believe that most of us would agree that the most significant and satisfying growth experiences we have had as members of organizations or even in our personal lives required a certain measure of risk.

Unfortunately, it seems that in many organizations today risk takers are an endangered species. I've studied and observed leadership in dozens of organizations over the years, and I am convinced that true risk-taking behavior is rare. I suppose that, in some ways, true risk-taking behavior in organizations is a little like a car accident. Like a car accident, risk-taking behavior can be dramatic and even traumatic. But unlike car accidents, risk-taking behavior is an extremely powerful and creative force that can breathe new life into stale, stolid, and worn-out organizations. Wheatley (1992) suggests that leaders need to be responsible inventors and discoverers. To accomplish this, however, leaders require the "courage to let go of the old world, to relinquish most of what we have cherished, to abandon our interpretations about what does and doesn't work" (p. 5). In other words, leaders need the courage to be risk takers.

Leadership roles today are not for the faint of heart. With all the inherent dangers of high-stakes testing and the extraordinary challenges imposed by sweeping federal legislative mandates such as the No Child Left Behind Act, our schools certainly don't need more leaders in search of safety! On the contrary, we need more true risk takers in our classrooms, administrative suites, and boardrooms. We need people in leadership roles with the courage of their convictions who will risk everything to live by their principles. In fact, I feel so strongly about the importance of courage in a leadership role that I often tell my students that people should never have jobs that they are afraid to lose.

I believe we need more leaders like the young Korean woman. She stood at the top of the pole that day and found the courage she needed in herself and the confidence she required in her teammates in order to take that risk and jump for the trapeze. She is a better person today for risking so much to conquer her fear, as are all of us who witnessed her courage. Maybe that's why she received more love and adoration from the group than anyone else who attempted the feat that day!

Do you have the courage that is required to lead? Are you inclined to be a risk taker? When did you last take that big gamble? Do you recognize that failure is a necessary facet of the innovative life? Can you live with the occasional failure in order to experience the exhilaration of jumping for the trapeze? Do you care enough about your purpose as a leader to forfeit a little safety for the opportunity to soar with the eagles?

TAKE TIME TO REFLECT

1. Think about a time in your life when you had to summon all the courage at your disposal to stand on top of the pole and jump for the trapeze in an attempt to do something that you were really afraid to do. What did you decide to do, and what were the results? Were the rewards worth the risks? If you had it to do over again, would you make the same decision? Why or why not?

2. All good leaders know that the willingness of people to take risks in order to change and grow is essential to the long-term welfare of any organization. There are a number of ways that leaders can encourage risk-taking behavior in their organizations. One way is to increase the rewards associated with taking risks, thereby making these behaviors more desirable. A second way to encourage risk-taking behavior is to minimize the threat of failure so that people aren't so afraid of failure that they won't even venture a risk. What are some of the ways that a leader can effectively increase the rewards associated with risk-taking behavior in his or her organization? What are some of the ways that a leader can reduce the fear of failure associated with taking risks?

CHAPTER THIRTEEN

WHO'S THE KING OR QUEEN OF THE JUNGLE?

I t was more than thirty years ago that I heard an amusing little story about status and what can happen to someone who takes his or her place in the pecking order too seriously. In all the years since, I've never forgotten that story. The story goes something like this.

One morning a big, old African lion awoke from a restful night of sleep feeling especially pleased with himself. Game had been plentiful of late, his hunts had been unusually successful, and he was growing stronger and fatter with each passing day. The lion slowly stretched and scratched a little itch on the back of his neck with one huge paw. He yawned a mighty yawn that reached clear to the depths of his aristocratic soul, and shook his great head from side to side in an effort to throw off the effects of his long, pleasant slumber.

While he was leisurely shaking his head in this way and rolling his long mane from side to side, he suddenly realized that he was thirsty. So, the lion decided that he would take a stroll down to a nearby watering hole and get a nice cool drink of water to quench his thirst. "Yes," he said to himself. "That will be the perfect way for me to start my day."

The lion gave his great, sleepy head one last big shake to get the cobwebs out and sauntered on down to the white sandy beach at the edge of the watering hole to get his drink. It was a pleasantly cool morning: The sun was shining brightly through the trees, birds were singing sweet songs all around him, and the air smelled fresh and clean. The lion decided that this day was indeed going to be glorious!

When the mighty beast arrived at the watering hole, he began to drink rapidly at first, then more slowly and leisurely as he felt his thirst subside. As the lion drank the sweet, cool water, he couldn't help but notice his reflection staring back at him from the surface of the crystal clear pool. He marveled at his grand countenance. He couldn't help but admire his many regal assets. He was greatly pleased as he surveyed his fierce, long, white teeth; his piercing golden eyes; his rich, thick, full mane; and the tight mounds of huge muscles that rippled throughout his mighty chest.

Carefully studying his reflection in this way, it was impossible for the lion not to notice that he was truly a magnificent creature. But even while he was viewing the evidence of what a remarkable specimen he was, unpleasant thoughts began to creep into his psyche and intrude on his feelings of contentment. Deep in the inner recesses of his mind, the lion wondered if all the other animals realized and appreciated what a wonderful and magnificent creature he was. Did they all understand and would they readily acknowledge that he, the mighty lion, was the king of all the beasts?

The lion couldn't allow his glorious day to be ruined by such negative and distressing thoughts. He decided that he would find out right away just how the other animals felt and thereby put the matter to rest once and for all. The lion took one final admiring glance at his reflection in the water, then turned and stalked into the jungle. There was a sense of purpose in his steps. He was determined to remind the other animals that he, and he alone, was the true and rightful king of the jungle.

The first animal he met on his foray into the jungle was an unfortunate monkey, who was distracted by his efforts to break open a coconut on a rock and so had not noticed the lion's approach. Before he knew it, the lion had grabbed him around his skinny little neck in a viselike grip. The lion pulled the monkey up against him in a fearful embrace. "Foolish little monkey!" he bellowed. "Who is the king of the jungle?" Though frightened out of his wits, the monkey didn't hesitate in his reply. "Why you are, mighty lion! You are the king of the jungle!" "That's right, you little pipsqueak, and just be sure you don't forget it!" said the lion releasing the frightened little monkey with a satisfied snort.

The lion moved deeper into the jungle. There, he saw a giraffe eating leaves from the top of a Banyan tree. The lion got a running start, leaped up high into the air, and grabbed the giraffe around the neck with his saber-like claws while yanking the giraffe's head down to the ground in one smooth, powerful motion. The lion stared with a terrible intensity into the terrified, soft, brown eyes of the giraffe. "Answer this question correctly and I might decide to let you live, you big gawky freak," said the lion. "Who is the king of the jungle?" The giraffe's knees were shaking so hard he could barely stand, much less speak. It was only by summoning all his inner strength that the gentle giant was able to reply in a barely audible whisper, "Why you are, sir. Everyone knows that you are the king of the jungle." "Say it again, and this time say it louder!" demanded the lion. "Oh, mighty lion, please don't hurt me! You are the king of the jungle! Everyone knows that you are the king," responded the giraffe. "That's absolutely, 100 percent correct!" said the lion. "I am indeed the king of the jungle!" He released the giraffe, while cautioning him that he'd better not forget for a single moment that he, the mighty lion, was the one and only king of the jungle.

Although the mighty lion was feeling quite a bit better about himself by this time, he decided that he required just a little more assurance. As fate would have it, the next animal that the king of the beasts encountered along the way was an old bull elephant, who was busy scratching his backside against the rough bark of a convenient coconut tree. The lion surveyed the elephant and immediately made the decision that this would be the perfect confirmation of his superiority throughout the entire animal kingdom.

The lion marched defiantly up to the old elephant, who had his eyes closed and was clearly enjoying scratching himself by rhythmically moving his ample backside to and fro against the coconut tree in a kind of soothing dance. The lion grabbed the elephant by the trunk and jerked the great beast's head in a violent motion down to a place where the two animals were at eye level. The mighty lion roared as loudly as he could directly into the old elephant's ear, "Hey, you big, fat, dumb jerk! Who's the king of the jungle?" For a fleeting moment, genuine surprise was reflected in the huge elephant's squinty little eyes. Unfortunately for the king of the beasts, that look of surprise was quickly replaced by a look of rage. Before the lion could realize what was happening to him, the old bull elephant had wrapped his powerful trunk tightly around the big cat's midsection. He twirled the lion around and around over his huge, gray head until the lion was totally disoriented. Then the elephant pounded the lion against the coconut tree until the lion's body was one giant bruise. Finally satisfied that he had punished the lion sufficiently, the elephant threw the king of the jungle unceremoniously to the ground in a big heap.

The elephant returned to scratching himself on his favorite coconut tree, while the stunned king of the jungle slowly staggered to his feet while dusting himself off. He surveyed the elephant with a confused look on his regal face and muttered softly, "Well, you don't have to get mad just because you don't know the answer."

Of course the humor in this little story is focused on the inflated perception that the lion held regarding his superiority over the other creatures in the jungle, but the lion is not all that different from many who are in leadership roles in all kinds of organizations. How easy we make it for our leaders to feel as if they are kings or queens of the jungle. Leaders can be blinded by the trappings that frequently go hand in hand with higher rank. Bigger offices, expense accounts, travel budgets, personal secretaries, designated parking spaces, and increased compensation can all conspire to tell the leader that he or she is something extra special and deserves to be valued above others in the organization. Added to the problem are subordinates in the hierarchy who curry the leader's favor, actively seek his or her counsel in all matters great and small, and always defer to the leader's judgment on every issue. Given these conditions, it's easy for the leader to lose perspective and actually begin to believe that he or she is the king or queen of the jungle.

School leaders can never forget that schools are not jungles—at least they shouldn't be! But the reality is that school leaders are presently facing particularly difficult and challenging times in their efforts to build nurturing, supportive school cultures where teachers can teach and children can learn without the threat of fear or intimidation. Governmental mandates such as the No Child Left Behind Act, coupled with the demands placed on teachers and students by high-stakes testing, can readily serve to create a jungle-like atmosphere in schools where the strongest survive and prosper while the less strong are held up to ridicule and are ultimately doomed to failure. If our schools are to be successful, they must be nurturing and caring places where people willingly work together to serve the best interests of students. Perhaps more than any other type of organization, a school should be a place where people are both willing and able to make themselves vulnerable so that they as well as others can experience intellectual, social, and emotional growth. Even the most cynical among us would be forced to agree that one can't do these things very well in a jungle-like environment.

Leadership is never about ruling others; leadership is about serving others. De Pree (1989) perhaps put it best when he said that the art of leadership is "liberating people to do what is required of them in the most effective and humane way possible" (p. 1). In this way, leaders are, in fact, servants of their followers, in that they remove the obstacles that prevent their followers from working to the best of their abilities. Force, fear, and intimidation are not the least bit liberating. People cannot function well, and most certainly not to their maximum potential, when they can't feel safe and free from external threats. It is the leader's responsibility to help all those in the organization to be safe and to feel safe—to liberate them to do what is required of them in the most effective and humane way possible!

As far as rank and status are concerned, they have little to do with successful organizations. This is true because the leader can serve as the king or queen of the jungle only at the pleasure of those who are being served. As soon as the leader forgets this important lesson, it's just a matter of time until he or she receives a painful reminder. Leaders should never forget that the strongest people in any organization are also, at the same time, the most gentle and compassionate. Their strength doesn't come from rank and status, but from a strong inner core of fundamental values that is consistently validated through their daily deeds and actions while fulfilling their responsibilities to others. This kind of strength doesn't require external confirmation from others—it is self-evident. So be very careful oh ye mighty lions; there is a big herd of elephants waiting for you out there!

TAKE TIME TO REFLECT

Lions are able to rule the jungle because they are fearsome and powerful creatures and most of the other animals are in no position to challenge them. Some individuals in leadership roles do, in fact, rule their respective organizations as if they were lions. Their coworkers allow them to rule because, like the jungle creatures in the story, they are also not in any position to challenge them. But all good leaders know that fear and intimidation are poor substitutes for genuine leadership. Identify some ways that you as a leader can effectively influence others in a positive direction without resorting to the use of fear and intimidation.

CHAPTER FOURTEEN

"HONEY, DO THESE PANTS MAKE ME LOOK FAT?"

U p until this point, the questions posed to the reader have been relatively easy. But prepare yourself, because that's about to change. "Honey, do these pants make me look fat?" is precisely the kind of question that has the potential to make you place your hands over your ears and run out of the room screaming. This is a question that no sane person ever wants to answer.

Just what makes this question so impossible? The question is impossible because by choosing an answer, we are forced to also choose between two competing outcomes that are both highly desirable. On one hand, most of us value the truth, and even if the truth is not particularly pretty, it's still the truth. So, if we are inclined to answer truthfully, the response might go something like this: "Fat's not the word! Those pants make you look enormous!" (We're being really truthful in this instance.) By answering truthfully, we are able to preserve our integrity, but, at the same time, we risk hurting the feelings of someone we may care for a great deal, and in the process we may even seriously damage an important relationship. So, in this instance, we might disdain the truth and choose an answer that is decidedly short on honesty but long on sensitivity, such as, "Wow! Sweetheart! You look absolutely fabulous in those pants! In fact, I believe they are slimming on you!" (We're being extremely sensitive here.) While this answer earns zero points for integrity, it does promote warm fuzzy feelings and helps to preserve blissful harmony in an important relationship.

So, what's the best answer to the question, "Honey, do these pants make me look fat?" I suppose that depends on a lot of variables that are highly idiosyncratic to each particular situation. When we can, most of us probably frame an answer somewhere in the middle of the two extremes I have proposed above. For example, "Sweetheart, I'm such a poor judge of fashion. All I know is that you look beautiful to me no matter what you are wearing!" might be a reasonable choice. With this answer, we try to preserve a little integrity balanced with a bit of compassion—and then ask for forgiveness when we say our prayers at the end of the day. (I suppose that I should admit that answers of this nature have made it possible for my wife and me to stay happily married for almost forty years. She frequently tells me what I want to hear!)

Unfortunately, many times there is no middle ground when making decisions in an organizational setting. We must choose one outcome or the other, because to compromise would result in the loss of both desirable outcomes. In the never-ending battle to build and maintain ethical and caring organizations, the challenge isn't related so much to the constant struggle to decide between right and wrong. The choices are relatively easy in those instances where we are able to differentiate right from wrong. In those instances, we simply choose to do what is right. However, as illustrated in the example above, the more difficult ethical challenge involves making choices between two mutually exclusive outcomes, both of which are highly desirable. These choices between right and right create moral dilemmas for caring leaders.

When I was serving as a school principal, I always took responsibility for the preparation of the master schedule. I reserved this responsibility for myself because I was pretty well convinced that a smoothly functioning school revolved around a well-conceived master schedule. Besides, I was a certified control freak at that time in my life, and I didn't have the capacity to trust this task to anyone else. So each spring, I would meet with each of the department chairs in turn, in the big conference room located at the rear of the administrative suite. There, we would arrange and rearrange courses on a big pegboard until we arrived at the master schedule we felt would work best for our students, our teachers, and ultimately, our school.

One year, we hired a new language arts teacher who had just completed an MA degree in American Literature. Because Jane was a new teacher and had a real strength in the area, the chair of the Language Arts department and I agreed that her teaching assignment should include several sections of American

Literature. The only problem with this decision was that Neal, one of the most senior teachers on the staff, had traditionally taught all the sections of American Literature for as long as anyone could remember.

In fact, when Neal reviewed the schedule, he couldn't believe his eyes. Who was this "Jane" person who was intruding on his domain? As soon as he recovered enough from the shock of seeing several sections of *his course* next to someone else's name, he made straight for my office. Neal was pretty intense when he stormed into the room. As I remember it, smoke was billowing out of both ears. He walked right up to my desk and pounded on it with his fist for emphasis. "Why are you giving *my course* to someone else?" he demanded. "Well, Neal," I said, "we didn't give 'your course' to someone else. We made a decision to divide the American Literature sections between you and Jane." "Oh no, you don't!" Neal shouted. "I am the American Literature teacher in this school! I teach all the sections of American Literature!"

I did my best to explain our reasoning for splitting the American Literature sections. I told Neal that because Jane was new to the teaching profession, we needed to do all that we could to provide her with an assignment that would help to ensure her a successful first-year experience. I also explained that, as a veteran teacher, we felt that Neal could easily make the needed adjustments to handle a more varied teaching assignment than he had been given in the past. "Besides," I told him, "it's good to try something new once in a while. It helps keeps one energized and fresh."

But Neal didn't want to be energized and fresh! He wanted to teach five sections of American Literature! He persisted, and insisted that I change his teaching assignment. Finally, when he wasn't able to get the answer he wanted from me, he played his trump card. "I thought you were my friend," he said. "I am your friend, Neal," I assured him. "But I'm also the principal of the school, and I have to make the decisions that I feel are best for our students and our school." With that, Neal turned on his heel and left my office. Thankfully, a week or so later, he stopped by the office again to let me know that although he still preferred to teach all the sections of American Literature, he understood the decision and was already working to prepare for his new assignment.

Putting aside the fact that I had handled the situation poorly in that I hadn't anticipated such a negative reaction from Neal and therefore hadn't made an effort to win him over before making my scheduling decision public, the question remained, Was this decision the right decision?

There were, of course, several desirable and undesirable outcomes on both sides of this issue. If I had let Neal have all the American Literature sections, he would no doubt have been pleased with his assignment. By honoring Neal's preference over the needs of a first-year teacher, I could have demonstrated my respect for seniority among the teaching staff, and Neal would have continued to think of me as a loyal, trustworthy, and caring friend. However, had I made that choice, I would have also done a disservice to our new teacher, Jane, by giving her an assignment that didn't play to her strengths. In doing so, I would have also ignored my responsibility to our students to give them the best possible teacher in every classroom, because Jane was unquestionably the better prepared of the two to teach American Literature, despite Neal's rather impressive record of longevity as The Teacher of that course.

Again, it's not a simple question of right versus wrong. The kinds of dilemmas that all leaders face as they make hundreds of routine and not-so-routine decisions on a daily basis invariably pit a wide range of values against each other. And if leaders don't know the relative place of competing values in their own personal value systems, then they are vulnerable to the urge to substitute others' values in place of their own when the going gets a little rough.

The choice to divide the American Literature sections between Neal and Jane was a relatively simple decision for me to make, but many of the choices facing leaders every day in all kinds of organizations are anything but simple. For example, should a younger, more talented employee be promoted over a highly committed, veteran employee who has given many years or valuable service to the organization? Obviously, there are any number of positive and negative implications, regardless of which choice the leader ultimately makes in this situation.

But one thing is clear. The most difficult decisions force leaders to choose not between right and wrong, but between right and right. As Badaracco (1997) has pointed out, in such circumstances, it is extremely difficult for leaders to know

> what to do when one clear right thing must be left undone in order to do another or when doing the right thing requires doing something wrong. . . . The right versus right problems typically involves choices between two or more courses of action, each of which is a complicated bundle of ethical responsibilities, personal commitments, moral hazards and practical pressures and constraints. (p. 6)

If we can think of these moral dilemmas as caused by a whole series of choices of right versus right, then a lengthy list of considerations presents itself. When it comes to decisions between right and right, we must recognize that there is typically no black and white, but plenty of gray. For example, when deciding an issue of right versus right, rather than asking ourselves if a particular course of action is right or wrong, we might do well to ask ourselves whether the course of action taken will be fair and just to all concerned, personally satisfying, self-promoting, culturally acceptable, or individually acceptable. We may also want to question whether or not the decision or action will produce the greatest utility, minimize harm, violate a written or unwritten contract, meet an obligation, or violate a spoken or unspoken promise. We may even need to decide whether, if given the opportunity, we would take the same action again. We might even do well to ponder the likelihood of our peers taking the same action if they were presented with a similar set of circumstances. For most right versus right decisions, some of the answers to the series of questions and considerations posed above will be ethically desirable, whereas others will be ethically undesirable. Regardless of the course of action taken, we simply can't expect to do everything right. We will leave some right things undone so that we can do others and do some things wrong as a consequence of doing something else right.

Badaracco (1997) warns all those who would attempt to lead that right versus right decisions reveal values, test commitment, and shape the future of the organization. Because so many values are in competition with each other, leaders are forced to prioritize their values (and clearly define the values of their organizations) when faced with making right versus right decisions. This prioritization process will test the leader's commitment to a value system, because many times the choices are extremely difficult. Making these difficult choices lets everyone know whether a leader can "walk the talk" when put to the test. Badaracco cautions that right versus right decisions are extremely critical to the long-term welfare of an organization because they have the capacity to shape the future of that organization by setting parameters for how future decisions are likely to be made. This phenomenon, which Badaracco has termed "shadowing forward," often leads to what he calls "defining moments" (p. 6) in the life of the leader and the organization, and these moments serve as "crucibles of character" (p. 4) as they test and mold the character of the leader.

When making extremely difficult right versus right decisions, how can leaders determine the correct thing to do? Since it's simply not acceptable to "cut the baby in half" and give one-half to each mother, how can leaders know who gets the whole baby? Can leaders afford to fudge on their priorities when making right versus right decisions and still maintain the high degree of integrity required to lead effectively? What happens to organizations when leaders fail to maintain respect for the values that define the mission? And finally, be honest: "Do these pants make me look fat?"

TAKE TIME TO REFLECT

1. Think of an occasion when you had to make a right versus right decision. What was the nature of the decision? What values were in competition? What did you ultimately decide? If you had it to do again, would you make the same decision today? Why or why not?

2. Are there ever instances when friendship or loyalty can or should trump a leader's responsibility to the organization? Should talent or qualifications always rank higher on the values meter than seniority? When making decisions, is respect for the individual as important as the consequences of that decision to the organization? Why or why not?

CHAPTER FIFTEEN

CAN I CARE ENOUGH
TO DO THE LITTLE
THINGS?

We can do no great things, only small things with great love.

—Mother Teresa

More than thirty years ago, I received an invitation to attend the Tournament Players Golf Championship in Florida. Because I like golf (even though golf apparently doesn't like me) and had never been to a big professional tournament before, I was genuinely excited by the opportunity. I got up before the crack of dawn that first morning of the tournament and drove to the course. I arrived at the tournament site well before the gates were opened to spectators because I didn't want to miss a single moment of the action.

The first players out on the course that morning are known as "rabbits" in the parlance of the golfing profession. I'm not sure why they are called rabbits, but it has something to do with the fact that they are not among the elite group of about 150 or so players who are exempt from qualifying for tournaments each week based on their official earnings from the tournaments they competed in during the previous year. Because rabbits have not won enough money (some haven't won any) to be in the exempt group of touring professionals, they have to compete with each other before the start of the regular tournament each week to earn one of very few remaining places in the tournament field. In effect, rabbits have to play an unofficial tournament, and play quite well, just to get into the field for the official tournament. Perhaps these players are called rabbits because they hop around the country from tournament site to tournament site each week, hoping to qualify for a chance to win big money in a Professional Golfers Association tour event. Unfortunately, most rabbits win little money, if any, and eventually most of them simply hop their way into golf obscurity.

I was out on the course as an observer early that first morning as the rabbits made their way around the golf course. The thing I remember most is the wonderful skills these nonexempt players, these golfing vagabonds, exhibited as they played their shots. Their drives were long and straight. Their short games were models of skill and precision as they nestled their iron shots mere feet from the pins. The touch they displayed on their putts would have made a skilled surgeon turn green with envy. In short, the rabbits were wonderful players in every respect. As I watched them display their marvelous skills, what amazed me most was that these players didn't make any money playing golf! That's why they were rabbits. If they had made a reasonable amount of money through their play, they would have been included among the exempt players.

Later that morning and into the afternoon, I watched the exempt players as they played their way around the course. Like the rabbits that had played ahead of them, they, too, possessed extraordinary skills that they displayed time after time with their powerful drives and precision shots. Just by watching, I could not distinguish any real differences between the rabbits and the exempt players. I saw some of the greatest players in the world that day, including Arnold Palmer, Jack Nicklaus, Lee Trevino, and Gary Player, but I could not distinguish just what it was that made their golf games superior to the golf games played by the rabbits.

When I thought more about it, I was drawn to the conclusion that the difference between worldwide fame and fortune as a professional golfer and total obscurity is very slight indeed. In fact, the difference is so small as to be virtually imperceptible to the naked eye. Yet however small that difference might be, it is quite real! In fact, it has proven to be real enough to make or break countless golfing careers over many years.

Since my trip to the Tournament Players Championship that day many years ago, I have reached two important conclusions. The first is that it is always a good idea to wear sunscreen when spending an entire day on a golf course in

Florida. This I learned the hard way. The second conclusion is that it is always the little things, and not the big things, that ultimately determine the winners and losers—not just in golf, but in leadership roles, and in just about anything else one attempts to master in life.

Why are the little things so important to success? The answer is that the margin between success and failure in almost any undertaking is always slight. No matter what challenges people are attempting to master, everyone will do the big things, but only those with a high level of commitment will devote the extra time and exert the extra effort necessary to do the little things, too. The big things are required if you are to be a player in any of life's games. If you want to be a professional golfer, for example, you have to show up at your appointed tee time with the correct number of clubs in your bag. Once on the course, you must obey the rules of the game. There are no exceptions: this is a BIG THING! Everyone who wishes to compete must obey the rules of the game! Those who fail to obey the rules of the game may be severely penalized or even disqualified.

But simply obeying the rules of the game won't make you a winner because everyone will be doing exactly what you are doing in this respect. If you wish to be successful, especially if you wish to be a winner, then you must do more. In fact, you must do much more.

In addition to his physical gifts, Jack Nicklaus has been widely acknowledged for his tremendous work ethic. In addition to devoting countless hours to practicing in preparation for tournaments, Nicklaus has always been considered one of the great students of the game. Nicklaus himself, for example, has often said that his head, not his physical prowess, was his biggest advantage in golf. While he clearly had great athletic ability, so did many of his competitors. But Nicklaus studied courses tirelessly and plotted strategies for how he would attack each hole. He was then very precise and disciplined in executing his strategy. In his efforts to prepare himself to succeed, Nicklaus was clearly superior to most of his competitors, and this was what provided him the tiny margin he needed to be successful where others failed. Consequently, his record in winning major championships stands alone and Jack Nicklaus is still regarded by many to be the greatest player ever in the long and storied history of golf. (Of course I realize that Tiger Woods could well change all that with his brilliant play.)

Consider, for a moment, just what it means to be the best at anything. For example, what does it means to be or to have a best friend? The term *best friend* certainly means better than average. It even means better than good— much better than good. The word *best* means most excellent, unsurpassed, preeminent, or paramount! But what is it about a best friend that makes that person most excellent, unsurpassed, preeminent, and paramount in that role?

A person is certainly not a best friend just because he or she does or says what's expected of a friend in ordinary or even extraordinary situations or circumstances. A person earns the mantle of best friend because that person consistently goes beyond what is expected and frequently does the unexpected in ordinary and extraordinary situations and circumstances.

Suppose, for a moment, that it is your birthday. Many people, including your best friend, may give you cards and even gifts on your birthday. But of course, that's expected—after all, it's your birthday! But what about all those days when it's not your birthday? What about that one particular day when nothing is going right and you're really feeling down, but nobody seems to care or even to notice your distress—nobody, that is, except your best friend.

Your best friend, who is always sensitive to your moods, will notice and may soothe you with some carefully chosen words of encouragement. Or perhaps she or he may send you flowers or take you out to dinner just to cheer you up. It is precisely this kind of commitment and caring expressed for you—not just on your birthday, but every day throughout the year—that makes your best friend so special. It is the willingness to go beyond what is ordinarily expected. It is going that extra mile, doing the little things that exhibit extraordinary caring and commitment to your well-being, that make your best friend most excellent, unsurpassed, preeminent, and paramount rather than just average or good in the role of friend. By the same token, it is the willingness of people to go beyond what is ordinarily expected in any endeavor that allows them to become most excellent, unsurpassed, preeminent, and paramount—in other words, to be the very best at whatever it is they are attempting to do.

In all the years that I have studied and observed leaders and leadership, I don't think I've have ever known a highly successful leader who was preeminent in her or his field over an extended period who failed to pay great attention to the little things. But I do know many successful leaders in a lot of different fields whose careful attention to the little things set them apart from their peers. If you think about the successful leaders you have known in schools, business, politics, coaching, or any field you care to name, I think you will agree that this is so.

I have yet to visit a school where the school leaders didn't have some means to organize students and teachers, a curriculum in place, textbooks and materials available, established policies and procedures for dealing with daily school life, and so forth. Those are big things, and they are required of all schools. Just because all those things are in place, though, doesn't demonstrate that a school has reached a high level of caring for students. I've never seen a teacher who didn't regularly open the door for his or her students to enter the classroom in the morning, who didn't try to deliver some kind of knowledge to the students in one way or another, or who failed to assign work for the students and give some kind of grade at the end of the marking period. These are not matters of choice—these are not little things, they are big things. These are fundamental things required of all teachers.

I have yet to experience a total school or even a classroom, for that matter, where the big things made a real difference in terms of the overall quality of the educational experiences that children received. It's always the little things that set schools and classrooms apart and make them exceptional places for children to be. But exactly what are those little things? What makes them so special?

When I first became a high school principal, I decided that I needed to do some things to demonstrate my caring and commitment to the students, the teachers, and the community. I thought it would be a good idea to single out some of the children who were experiencing academic and behavioral problems at school and visit them in their homes. Each week, I selected a child who was having a particularly difficult time at school and dropped by his or her home in the afternoon. These visits were always unannounced. I would just drive up to the kid's place of residence, get out of my car, go inside, and visit with whomever was available and had a vested interest in the kid's future. Sometimes I would catch a mother cooking dinner while preparing to go to a second job later that evening. The house might be in total disarray, and someone might even be passed out drunk on the couch. In such instances, I would sit on a stool in the kitchen and talk with the mother about her child while she cooked. At other times, when I arrived at the kid's house, there might not be a father or a mother, but a grandmother who had taken on the responsibility of raising her grandchildren. If that were the case, then I would sit with that grandmother on a sofa in the living room and talk about what we could do together to help her grandchild succeed in school.

No matter what the circumstances were in the home, the trip was always worthwhile for two reasons. The first was that my willingness to go into the community and talk about the child's educational problems rather than asking the community to come to me at the school was tangible evidence that I cared about the children in my school. It was evidence that I cared even about those children who were doing poorly or who were troublesome. Most people would probably agree that my job as a principal didn't require me to go to children's homes and visit with their families after work. After all, home visits were not specifically included in my official job description. I went to visit children's homes not because I had to, but because I wanted to demonstrate that I cared about the children. And I did care about them!

The second reason that the trips were worthwhile was that they revealed to me in bold and living color the kinds of home environments that some of our struggling students were forced to deal with in their everyday lives. Sometimes I was shocked by what I saw, but I needed to be shocked. It made me more sensitive and empathetic toward these students; it allowed me to be more patient with them as I worked with faculty and staff to seek solutions to their educational problems.

Given the broad range of responsibilities I had as principal of the school, my weekly visits in the community were small things. They were so small, in fact, that, as I've noted, they weren't specifically included in my job description. Nobody ever asked me about them. Nobody even knew that I made these visits, with the exception of those kids and their families who were the recipients of my unexpected social calls. But I am convinced that my home visits were some of the more important things that I did, because they were highly visible signs for our children and their caretakers of my commitment to those students who were experiencing difficulties in our school.

Several years ago, one of my closest friends and colleagues lost his father after an extended illness. The funeral was scheduled for the middle of the week at a site about nine hundred miles round trip from where I lived at the time. At first, I thought I would purchase a really nice funeral spray and send it to express my family's sympathy, but not attend the funeral because of the time and travel involved. This would have been the expected thing for me to do in this circumstance, given the great distance that would have to be traveled to attend the funeral, the fact that the funeral was being held in the middle of the work week, and how busy my work schedule was at the time. On further reflection, however, I decided that I should take a few days and drive to the funeral because I knew that my presence there would mean a great deal to my friend. I didn't tell my friend of my plans to attend the funeral of his father because, had he known of my plans to attend, he would have tried to discourage me from making the trip. He knew how busy I was at the time, and he's the kind of person who always puts the needs of others ahead of his own.

At any rate, I made the trip and arrived at the funeral chapel shortly before the appointed time. When my friend came out into the chapel and saw me, he didn't have to say anything—I could tell from the expression on his face that he was moved by my presence there. My presence touched him because he hadn't expected me to come, but I had come anyway. The fact that I had made the decision to attend the funeral certainly wasn't a big thing by any stretch of the imagination, but it would be hard for anyone to deny that it was a very significant thing, at least from my friend's perspective. It was significant because it demonstrated in an unmistakable way that I had a very high level of caring for his well-being.

The day after my friend returned to work after attending his father's funeral, he again thanked me for taking the time and driving all that distance to show my support for him. My reply to his expression of gratitude was simply this: "Life affords us too few opportunities to show others how much we care. We simply can't afford to waste those opportunities." I don't know about you, but I don't want to waste any of those precious opportunities to show others who are very special to me just how much I care.

Each summer, the department of education at our university sponsors an institute for teacher leaders in Southern California. The institute is a powerful expression of the University of La Verne's commitment to the professional development of teachers in the region. Although I think that the entire institute is a truly wonderful event, I am particularly fond of one of the activities that is always a part of the experience. On the last day of the institute, each participant is presented with a beautiful crystal apple. Although the apples are presented to the participants, they aren't for them to keep. Each person must in turn give the apple to a teacher from his or her past. It must be presented to someone whose influence was of great significance in that individual's personal and professional growth and development. I've often wondered what it must feel like for a teacher to unexpectedly receive the gift of one of those apples. The apple is rather small in terms of its dollar value, but is enormous in terms of the personal validation it can bestow on a recipient.

Successful leaders recognize and appreciate the importance of the impact that little things can have on the overall health and vitality of an organization. They realize that by going beyond broad expectations and demonstrating commitment through performing small but significant acts of caring, they can build an environment that will bring out the best in everyone. For example, I know outstanding leaders who spend hours and hours acknowledging contributions of others in the organization through hand-written notes, e-mails, or personal telephone calls. I have even known some who visit all their employees once each year at their job sites to thank them for the contributions they are making and to remind them of the importance of the work they are doing to the overall success and well-being of the organization. I know leaders who regularly bring flowers from home to brighten up the work environment, and others who take the time to learn not just the names of all their employees, but also other personal information such as where they are from or some of the details about their families. None of these little acts of caring is required, but good leaders know very well that such acts of caring can make a difference in any organization.

It is the leader who is willing to go beyond what is required and do the little things, those things that are essentially voluntary, who will always gain the edge in meeting the challenges of leadership. One can never expect to be the best leader he or she can be simply by playing by the rules of the game and doing what is expected—he or she must do more. Remember, success in any endeavor is highly discriminating and always favors those who are willing to go the extra mile—those who demonstrate an uncommonly high level of commitment and caring through their willingness to do more than is absolutely necessary to meet the basic requirements associated with a particular role.

When it comes to providing effective leadership, how do you feel about the importance of the so-called little things? Is it your goal to be good? Better? Best? Do you believe in going that extra mile? Have you demonstrated to others for whom you have leadership responsibility how much you care through little acts of thoughtfulness, or have you wasted those precious opportunities? What are some of the little things that you can do in your present work environment to demonstrate your caring? What are you waiting for?

TAKE TIME TO REFLECT

1. Suppose you were given the opportunity to show your caring through the presentation of a token of appreciation such as a beautiful crystal apple to someone who has been a special mentor in your life. To whom would you give that token of appreciation, and why would she or he be selected? What did that person do for you that made her or him so significant in your life?

2. Write a letter to the person you selected above acknowledging his or her contributions to your growth as a leader and a person and mail it to it her or him or take that person to lunch and express your gratitude in person.

3. What kind of "little things" are you doing to make your leadership special to those you are presently serving in a leadership role? What are some other little things that you can do to make your attitude of caring felt by those whom you are serving?

CHAPTER SIXTEEN

"CAN YOU JUST CALL ME WILLIE, MRS. PETERSON?"

Acouple of years ago, I attended a meeting of independent college deans in Sacramento. Being the compulsive person that I am, I flew up the evening before the meeting to avoid the hassle of a very early morning flight the day of the meeting and the compulsory rush-hour traffic jam on the ride into the city from the airport. I absolutely hate to be late to meetings, and besides, I've learned that going a little early allows for some reflective time one might not ordinarily get the opportunity to enjoy.

While I was leisurely sipping my coffee in the hotel room on the morning of the meeting, I picked up a complimentary copy of an *Esquire* magazine that had been placed on the coffee table. This particular issue contained a series of interviews with athletes and other celebrities focusing on the important lessons they had learned in life. I have to admit that I was fascinated by the experiences these famous folks had to share and the wisdom gleaned from living a life in the spotlight of public opinion. While I'm admitting, I'll also admit that I read the interviews with several of the supermodels. Some of them, such as Lauren Hutton, had some very interesting insights to share and they did it in a surprisingly articulate manner. But then, wouldn't any reasonable person have to agree that a pretty face doesn't necessarily imply an empty head?

I suppose I read a dozen or more of the interviews before I left for my meeting that morning, but one interview stood out from all the rest in terms of its impact on me. That interview was with the former heavyweight boxing champion of the world, the indomitable Muhammad Ali. In the interview, Ali recalled a life-changing experience he had had in his hometown of Louisville, Kentucky, after winning the light heavyweight boxing gold medal for the United States at the 1960 Olympics:

> I came back to Louisville after the Olympics with my shiny gold medal. Went into a luncheonette where black folks couldn't eat. Thought I'd put them on the spot. I sat down and asked them for a meal. The Olympic champion wearing his gold medal. They said, "We don't serve niggers here." I said, "That's okay. I don't eat 'em." But they put me out in the street. So I went down to the river, the Ohio River, and threw my gold medal in it. (Fussman, 2004, p. 88)

Can you imagine for just a moment that, through your own hard work, sacrifice, and commitment, you have accomplished something as wonderful and remarkable as winning an Olympic gold medal? Here you are, back in the bosom of your old hometown, the place where you were raised. You are universally acknowledged as the very best light heavyweight amateur boxer in the entire world and nobody—nobody outside your own friends and family—recognizes your accomplishment. The only thing that people acknowledge about you is the color of your skin. Can you imagine how dehumanizing that experience must have been for Muhammad Ali?

I must confess that I, for one, cannot even begin to imagine what it would feel like to experience an incident as humiliating and dehumanizing as Ali lived through that day in Louisville! But clearly it must have hurt Ali terribly for him to throw his hard-earned Olympic gold medal into the Ohio River. And most likely, it had a profound impact on his life from that point forward. After reading about his experience in that Louisville restaurant in 1960, I understood much better why Muhammad Ali refused induction when he was drafted into the military several years later during the Vietnam War. Ali's refusal to accept induction into the military angered many Americans at the time and he was severely criticized for his unwillingness to serve "his country." He was even sentenced to a prison term that was later overturned because of his conscientious objector status. But religious considerations aside, why would anyone in his right mind willingly lay his life on the line for a country that totally and completely rejected his humanity?

I grew up in a small town in northeast Florida during the 1950s and 1960s. Although I completed my formal public school education about ten years after

Brown v. Board of Education (1954), I never went to school with a black child. What's more, I never really knew any black people while I was growing up. I can't recall ever having a discussion or even a polite conversation with a black person until I joined the United States Navy after graduation from high school in 1963.

Everything in my hometown was separate for blacks and whites, from water fountains to restrooms to restaurants to schools—separate, but certainly not equal. For example, black patrons were restricted to the balcony seats at the local movie theater, they were obliged to ride in the back of city buses, and their neighborhoods were confined to easily identifiable pockets in the poorer sections of the town. Thinking back, where black people lived was just about the only thing I had in common with them.

My mother had divorced my alcoholic father when I was still a small child. There were few job opportunities for women at that time, and even if there had been, she had no special training or skills that would have qualified her for a good job, so she worked as a waitress at a restaurant in town. After her divorce, her lack of financial resources forced her to move with my sister and me to live with my grandmother in a small, wood-frame house without indoor plumbing on the west side of town. The street where I lived butted up against a black neighborhood. I saw black people passing on the street by my grandmother's house, coming and going to the grocery store or to work, just generally carrying on the business of living their daily lives. But I never spoke a word to the black people who passed along the edges of my tiny world, or even acknowledged their existence. Truthfully, because of all the things I had heard about them, I was pretty much intimidated by black people when I was a small child.

When I was growing up, everything that I thought I knew about race and social class was what I learned from my grandmother and my uncles, aunts, and cousins. They were the most significant people in my world when I was a child. The "n-word" was frequently used by those around me to denote black people. It seems inconceivable to me now, but as a small child, I had no idea that the term was derogatory. In fact, it was used so often, so casually, and seemingly without rancor in a totally matter-of-fact manner that, as a child, I honestly thought the term was merely descriptive, such as New Yorker, South American, or Baptist.

When I was about three or four, I would spend many Saturday afternoons with my uncles and their drinking buddies at Ashton's grocery store on the corner, just up the street from my grandmother's house. There, while we listened to country music on the radio for hours on end, my uncles sat in wooden rocking chairs, drank Miller High Life beer, and discussed the events of the day with their cronies. The lives and habits of black people were a frequent topic of conversation. I heard over and over again that black people were "no account and lazy" and that they didn't take care of the children that resulted from their indiscriminate sex. I had the impression from listening to my uncles and their buddies that most black people relied on welfare checks to survive, and that they routinely squandered those checks during drinking binges, when they fought and cut each other up with razors.

It seems ironic to me now to realize that my uncles and their friends had a lot in common with the people they were gossiping about. For the most part, the people who shaped my early views on race and social class were themselves poorly educated, blue collar workers struggling mightily just to get by in the world. I suppose that my uncles and their friends made themselves feel better by putting down blacks, who were struggling just as hard, if not harder, to make some kind of decent life for themselves and for their families. And, of course, the black people in town had the added burden of racial injustice with which they had to deal just to get a shot at something better.

After a time, my grandmother fell ill and was unable to care for my sister and me while my mother was at work. Because we were too young to be left alone, my mother was forced to place us temporarily in the Junior House, which was the county home for orphans and other children who had no one who was willing or able to care for them.

The time I spent at the Junior House was, without question, the most miserable period in my life. My mother and her boyfriend, who would later become my stepfather, dropped my sister and me at the Junior House the day after Christmas in 1949. I was four years old. My sister and I didn't know that we were going to the Junior House when we got into the car that day, and when we got there, we had no idea how long we would remain. We were just dropped off along with our clothes and a couple of our favorite toys. I remember being confused when I found out that I couldn't leave with my mother when she drove away in the car that day. I still recall what it was like to go to bed every night and wake up every morning feeling afraid, unloved, unworthy, insignificant, and powerless.

It wasn't until many years later that I recalled an incident that I experienced during one of my first days at the Junior House that typified what it was like for me to be a small child in a hostile environment with absolutely no control over any aspect of my own life. We were having dinner one evening, and I reached for a slice of bread from the top of a stack on a plate that included almost a whole loaf of bread. While reaching for the single slice of bread at the top of the stack, I accidentally touched the slice below. The woman who managed the Junior House was absolutely incensed by my apparent lack of manners. In order to teach me a lesson that I would never forget, she made me eat the entire loaf of bread. That was a lot of bread for a four-year-old and it took a long time and a lot of tears to get through the entire loaf. But it was indeed a lesson I never forgot, although I did repress the event for many years. Because of that lesson and others like it, I will never forget what it feels like for a human being to have absolutely no control over his or her life, to be essentially powerless. I will never forget what it feels like to be called to the front of a first-grade classroom to receive a free lunch ticket, or to wear shirts made out of Purina chicken feed sacks. In all honesty, I never want to forget, either.

I don't remember just how long my sister and I stayed at the Junior House, if it was months or a year or more. Later, when I was older and curious about my early life, my mother was never predisposed to discuss those times. But looking back, I am truly grateful for those early experiences. I am grateful because I feel that these experiences helped me transcend the ignorance and hateful arrogance that typified my early environment. Being a ward of the Junior House was one of the best things that ever happened to me because it taught me what it felt like to be stripped of one's dignity and sense of worth as a human being. At the very least, the Junior House experience helped me empathize with and be an advocate for others who have suffered similar circumstances through no fault of their own, circumstances that may have set them apart as social outcasts in one way or another.

The most remarkable thing to me now is that, during all the time I was growing up in the South, I never once questioned the social order. Like just about everyone else at the time, I became acclimated to the conditions. I assumed that things were the way they were supposed to be. No one I respected or admired or loved ever questioned the way things were. In fact, everyone I knew thought that things were exactly as they should be—that God was in his heaven and all was right with the world, as Robert Browning put it. Of course, I didn't know any black people.

At this point in my life, I freely admit that I don't have the vaguest notion of what it was like to be black in the middle of the last century in this country. I don't know, because I have never had to drink from a blacks-only water fountain, been forced to ride at the back of the bus, been turned away from a restaurant because of my skin color, or been restricted to the balcony seating at the movie theater. I also admit that I don't know what it's like to be a woman, or a Jew, or anything else that I'm not now nor have ever been. In fact, I recognize that even at this point in my life, I'm probably still sexist and racist and prejudiced in some subtle ways. Although this may seem like a foolish thing for me to admit, I believe it's an extremely important admission, because I can't begin to address my shortcomings as a human being and a leader unless I first acknowledge that these shortcomings may exist.

Perhaps the cartoon sailor, Popeye, put it best when he said, "I yam what I yam." Like everyone else, I am a product of my genetic inheritance coupled with all that I have learned and experienced in my lifetime—that is, of both nature and nurture. I believe I must acknowledge this truth and then work to overcome all the barriers that these circumstances have placed on me that prevent me from being able to relate in an honest and caring way with my fellow human beings, whether they be black or white, man or woman, Jew or Protestant. I'm not ashamed to admit that I probably have innate preju- dices. Regrettably, it is a natural tendency for human beings to identify most closely with others who are like them and to look with suspicion and distrust on those who are different. The more differences that exist, and the greater the degree of those differences, the greater the effort required to overcome them. But all of us who aspire to lead must make that effort!

In my opinion, it is the height of arrogance for anyone to think that one can put oneself in someone else's place and feel the things the other person feels. While we certainly can and should empathize with the circumstances and situations with which others are dealing, no matter how hard we may try we can't actually feel the same feelings. We all know people who say things like, "Oh, I know what it's like to be black," when they aren't black or "I know just how she must feel losing her child!" when they have never experienced this tragic circumstance in their own lives.

I have come to realize that we don't have a clue how others feel unless we have actually been in their shoes. This is an important realization for me and for any leader because it helps guard against considering the feelings of others too lightly, for carelessly assuming that we can know exactly how events and circumstances, or sometimes even a simple word or gesture, will affect others. The realization that we cannot know what it feels like to be white or black, a man or a woman, or a Jew or a Protestant unless we are those things should encourage us to seek to learn how and why others think, act, and feel as they do before we say things or take actions as leaders that may have deleterious effects on their humanity.

A good friend and colleague, J. David Smith, has suggested that preju- dice is a kind of disease that we catch from others. In his wonderfully heart- warming and insightful book, *In Search of Better Angels* (2003), Smith explains what he means when he says that prejudice is an illness:

> Prejudice is a form of mental illness—I'm convinced of it. Unfortunately, it is often a form of shared mania that results in great hurt to those who are objects of its madness. Most people with other forms of mental ill- ness are dangerous only to themselves. Prejudice is different. Its primary

symptom is hatred of others, and those who are hated are at high risk of being hurt. (p. 34)

Will we ever get beyond our differences to the point that these differences will no longer divide us, but will instead serve to make us stronger as a society? Although I don't expect to live long enough to see a utopian society free of prejudice, I am encouraged by the knowledge that we have grown significantly in our tolerance and, more importantly, by our acceptance and even celebration of our differences since Muhammad Ali hurled his Olympic gold medal into the Ohio River. Personally, I have great faith that we will continue to grow in this direction.

When I was doing my student teaching during the late 1960s, the black pride movement came into vogue. One day, my supervising teacher was discussing the movement with the students in one of our eighth-grade English classes. She admitted that she was a little confused by the whole black pride movement but wanted to be sensitive to the feelings of the black students in her classes. She asked a young man in the front row, "Willie, now tell me honestly, do you prefer to be called colored, or Negro, or black?" Without hesitation, the young man looked her straight in the eye and replied, "Can you just call me Willie, Mrs. Peterson?"

TAKE TIME TO REFLECT

1. Can you admit that in some respects, you may be racist, sexist, or perhaps prejudiced in some other way? Do you feel that this is an important admission for any leader? What have you done to help you better understand the thoughts and feelings of those who are not like you? What are you willing to do?

2. Working with a group of friends of colleagues, organize an exercise in which each of the group members assumes the viewpoint of someone very different in some essential respect. For example, if you are a young woman, you might choose to assume the vantage point an older man; if you're Caucasian, you may assume the role of an African American or a Latino. Once the members of your group have their assumed identities in place, then discuss and debate several important issues such as illegal immigration, affirmative action, or school vouchers from the perspective of your new vantage point. When you are done discussing issues, talk about how your assumed identity may have affected your views.

CHAPTER SEVENTEEN

HOW ARE SCHOOLS TRANSFORMED?

At the University of South Carolina, where I worked for many years, my colleagues and I engaged in a number of research projects over twenty years in an effort to understand how schools worked so that we could help make them better places for teachers to teach and children to learn. One of the primary areas of focus for our research efforts was compensatory education.

We selected compensatory education as a major focus for several reasons, including these: (1) A lot of resources are expended on compensatory education programs. (2) For the most part, compensatory programs have generally been regarded as largely ineffective. (3) A lot of children (especially in the South) were being served by these ineffective compensatory programs. (4) In general, those who are served by compensatory education can be categorized as low-achieving, low-socioeconomic-status students who don't have many advocates to represent their interests. Unlike special education students, who come from a variety of backgrounds that straddle the social strata, compensatory students come only from poor families. In our region, that generally meant poor, black families. In this country, as in most other countries in the world, *poor* is synonymous with *powerless*. For all these reasons, we thought we should try to help.

When we first began our study of compensatory programs, we were shocked and dismayed by what we found. About twenty years ago, my colleague, Lorin Anderson, directed a study of Chapter 1 schools in the region as a part of a reauthorization study for the federal government. As a part of the research design, members of his research team went into Chapter 1 schools and shadowed students in the program to try to understand what it was like to actually be a student in a Chapter 1 program. The researchers followed the children throughout all their activities during the day and noted the kinds of instructional experiences they were exposed to in a typical school day.

After a few weeks of gathering data in this way, Lorin brought his research team together in a meeting designed to let researchers share the early results of their efforts. One of the research team members began to report on the things she had been observing. The more she talked about what she had witnessed, the more emotional she became, until she was sobbing inconsolably. She was weeping for all the first- and second-grade children who were intellectually wasting away in Chapter 1 programs in the schools she had visited. She regarded these young children as already academically dead, doomed to a lifetime of failure in school and in life. She knew in her heart that these children were not getting the things they needed from their school experiences to allow them to live satisfying and productive lives, and it hurt her deeply.

These experiences with the Chapter 1 reauthorization study led us to conduct a large study of remedial and compensatory programs in South Carolina for the Education Improvement Act (EIA) Select Committee, a blue-ribbon oversight committee charged with monitoring the progress of the massive Education Improvement Act enacted by the general assembly in South Carolina in 1984. The state was expending considerable money on compensatory and remedial education and the select committee wanted to know what the people of South Carolina were receiving for their money.

Without going into detail, some of the results of our study were disturbing, if not downright shocking (Anderson, Cook, Pellicer, Sears, & Spradling, 1989). For example, we discovered that the standards that the state had set to judge whether individual schools were successful or unsuccessful in their compensatory programs were so low as to be meaningless. Under the state standards, to be successful a school had to achieve one normal curve equivalency (NCE) gain, on average, for two of three years on standardized tests in reading and math. Under these standards, approximately 95 percent of the compensatory math programs in South Carolina were judged successful by the state, while 90 percent of the compensatory reading programs were judged successful. When we reviewed the progress of students who had been placed in compensatory programs, however, we found that about two-thirds of them either spent their entire academic careers in compensatory programs or returned to them periodically throughout their school careers. Because the primary purpose of compensatory education is to give students the knowledge and skills they need to return to and remain in the academic mainstream, the numbers touting the resounding success of the South Carolina compensatory programs simply didn't add up. Based on this information, I asked the state superintendent of education a simple question: "How can 95 percent of the programs be successful, while two-thirds of the students are failures?" As you might suspect, this was not a question to which the chief state school officer cared to respond—so he didn't.

We found some other problems in the compensatory programs that we felt were significant and needed to be addressed. For example, when we analyzed the curricula being taught to students in compensatory programs, we found that students were being taught approximately two grade levels below those on which they were being tested with standardized tests. Consequently, even though students successfully passed their work in school, they were doomed to fail the standardized tests. Given these circumstances, it was little wonder that so few of them exited compensatory programs and returned to and remained in the academic mainstream.

Needless to say, the results of our study created quite a stir in the halls of government. The chief result of our painstaking work was that most of those connected with compensatory programs spent the majority of their efforts trying to save face rather than directing those efforts toward improving the programs. We were depressed by all this and decided that we would change our tack. Rather than studying programs that were unsuccessful, we would go in an entirely different direction and study some programs that were successful. This provided me with the rare opportunity to see something quite wonderful— schools that had been transformed!

When we reviewed the long-term compensatory test results for our state, we discovered that twelve schools and their students had made not just the one NCE gain that was the standard for success, but had made double-digit NCE gains in reading or math, or both, for three consecutive years. These were astounding results, more than ten times the standard that had been established to measure success! Of course, the big question that was begging to be answered was, "How did they do it?" We decided to find out.

After reviewing data on all twelve schools, we selected four schools for further study and sent teams of researchers to each of the four to observe in classrooms, conduct interviews, collect artifacts, and so forth. I was a member of the team that visited an elementary school I will call Zenia Elementary. Let me describe for you some of the things we saw and felt when we visited Zenia Elementary, a living example of a school that had been transformed.

When we entered the school for the first time, there was a special feeling that seemed to radiate from the building itself. It came from the hallways, the cafeteria, the office complex. The building seemed to be saying to us, "This is a different kind of school. Something special is going on here."

There was something in the air, but we didn't know exactly what it was. We could feel it, but we couldn't begin to decipher or even to describe it. Arranged on the walls on each side of the hallway, stretching from the front entrance to the main office area, were self-portraits of the children. All the faces seemed to be happy and smiling. The school's maintenance engineer greeted the research team at the entrance and escorted us to the administrative offices. He had been briefed and knew that we were coming, and he expressed his pleasure that we would be in *his* school for several days. He gave the impression that not only was he proud to be a staff member at Zenia, but also that he knew that he was fortunate to be a part of something special. This kind of feeling was subsequently reflected in conversations with all the staff members and most of the students we met during our school visit.

My initial encounter with the maintenance engineer, as well as my interactions with other staff members, reminded me of Wheatley's (1992) ideas concerning the existence of invisible fields in organizations that occupy all the space that appears to be empty to the naked eye. These fields are filled with tiny particles, or waves, or forces, like those found in magnetic fields or radio transmissions, for example. These invisible forces are present in the vacant spaces of organizations, and they constantly signal the vision that is the essence of the organization. Wheatley believes that everyone in the organization, whether consciously or unconsciously, is constantly sending out signals that serve to form these fields:

> Now, we need to imagine ourselves as broadcasters, tall radio beacons of information, pulsing out messages everywhere. We need all of us out there, stating, clarifying, discussing, modeling, filling all of space with the messages we care about. If we do that, fields develop—and with them, their wondrous capacity to bring energy into form. . . . If we have not bothered to create a field of vision that is coherent and sincere, people will encounter other fields, the ones we have created unintentionally or casually. It is important to remember that space is never empty. If we don't fill it up with coherent messages, if we say one thing but do another, then we create dissonance in the very space of an organization. (pp. 55–56)

There was no dissonance in the fields radiating throughout Zenia Elementary. Everyone was sending the same signals about the things they cared about most. We found out exactly what those things were in our first interview, which was conducted with the man who had been principal of the school for sixteen years.

The principal, whom I shall refer to as Dave, was a bundle of optimism, energy, and commitment. When we asked him to explain the extraordinary success of his school in educating compensatory youngsters, he thought about the question for a moment before he replied. Then he said, "When I became principal of this school sixteen years ago, I looked around me, and I didn't see a school for children. I said to the teachers, 'Do you want this to be a school for children? If you will help me, then we can make it so.'" He then proceeded to tell us how they had organized their compensatory program to make certain that children would be successful.

The keystone of their vision for children at Zenia Elementary was a simple declaration: *No child shall fail.* The administration, teachers, and staff had all bought into the notion that the school would have a zero tolerance for failure and that no child would be allowed to fail, no matter what the circumstances. Once this vision was firmly in place, the rest was almost easy.

Because compensatory students were the most academically needy students in the entire school, the decision was made that they should receive the best resources the school had to offer. That meant that the compensatory students would get the very best teachers, the most enriched curriculum, the finest materials and supplies, and the most desirable classrooms. To say the least, this is atypical of most of the compensatory programs with which I am familiar. At Zenia Elementary, it became a cherished honor among the faculty to be asked to teach the compensatory students, because only the very best teachers were entrusted with these children.

The year that we visited Zenia Elementary, 98 percent of the compensatory students from the previous year had tested out of the compensatory program by the end of the first grade, which was the grade level on which their program was focused. These incredible results can be put in perspective only when compared to a two-thirds failure rate for the state as a whole. But even more remarkable, not only did 98 percent of the compensatory students test out of the program, but their test scores fell at the midpoint or above in relation to all the students at their grade level who had been tested. This insulated them from the likelihood that they would fall back into the compensatory program at some later date in their school careers.

When the test results were received by the school and the principal announced them to the faculty and staff during a faculty meeting, the compensatory teachers received a standing ovation from their colleagues for the wonderful work they had done with their students. I admit it is difficult for me to imagine what it must feel like, what a marvelously confirming personal and professional experience it would be, for a teacher or anyone in any organization for that matter, to receive a standing ovation from his or her colleagues for outstanding contributions to the goals of the organization. When the applause died down, however, Dave said to those assembled, "Colleagues, we've done a wonderful job this past year. We achieved a success rate of 98 percent. But you know what? If we work just a little harder, I know that we can reach 99 percent!" He was simply reminding the staff that at Zenia Elementary School that the ultimate goal, *no child shall fail,* was still not fully achieved.

At Zenia Elementary, barriers that tended to isolate people from each other had been systematically removed. Interactions among students, teachers, administrators, parents, and citizens were frequent, varied, and were a two-way street. Student personnel teams comprised of administrators, teachers, counselors, and other specialists were regularly convened to try to come up with solutions for students experiencing difficulties at school. If you think about it, doctors don't work in isolation, and neither do attorneys or engineers—so why should teachers? At Zenia, everyone felt a joint responsibility to work with their colleagues to make sure that all students were successful. This should be true in every organization!

At Zenia, there was a powerful climate of caring that permeated the entire school. Teachers cared for students, and students cared for teachers. Administrators cared for students and teachers, and vice versa. Everything that was done with and for everyone in the school reflected that caring. A Love Jar was located in the main office to collect funds to provide children from impoverished families with things they needed. Staff members, children, and community members all made donations. Teachers didn't want to take their sick days even when they were ill because they felt as if their students and their colleagues needed them to be there every day. It was evident that the community cared about the school and the children who were served by the school. The school boasted more than three hundred active volunteers and thirteen corporate sponsors, all of whom provided a wealth of human and fiscal resources to enhance the programs at Zenia.

One of the most memorable interviews during my visit to Zenia was conducted with the school's media specialist. She told me that when the principal, Dave, had invited her to join the staff of the school a number of years before, she had initially declined his invitation. But Dave had persisted, and finally she told him, "Dave, I don't want to come to Zenia Elementary because I don't know anything about being an elementary school media specialist. I'm a high school media specialist." His reply to her declaration was telling: "I don't care about the things that you know and don't know—I care about the kind of person that you are. You are the kind of person I want to be our media specialist." So, against her better judgment, she agreed to accept the position of media specialist at Zenia. She told me how one day she had come into the media center and wondered how it looked to a first grader. She explained that, to find out, she got down on her knees and knee-walked around the entire media center to get the view from a first grader's perspective. I know why Dave hired this woman to be the media specialist at Zenia: She was exactly the kind of person who would joyfully share a vision that no child shall fail! In the words of Peter Senge (1990),

> A shared vision is not an idea. It is not even an important idea such as freedom. It is, rather, a force in people's hearts, a force of impressive power. It may be inspired by an idea, but once it goes further—if it is compelling enough to acquire the support of more than one person—then it is no longer an abstraction. It is palpable. People begin to see it as if it exists. Few, if any, forces in human affairs are as powerful as shared vision. (p. 206)

So what happens when a vision is shared by everyone in an organization? When people in an organization share a vision they become connected in a fundamental and essential way. The organization derives a unified sense of purpose from this connectedness, and the shared vision becomes a powerful force, a force capable of transforming almost any school into the kind of place that we all know it can and should be. At Zenia Elementary, that was a place where children were not allowed to fail. The power that can be derived from a shared vision makes it possible for those of us who work in organizations to deal with all the daily distractions that we routinely face, and at the same time, to make significant progress toward our common purpose. The common purpose is what allows people to be engaged with their work because that is what matters most to those who share a vision.

Sergiovanni (1992) has described the connectedness that results from a shared vision in terms of a learning community that "resembles what is found in a family, a neighborhood, or some other closely knit group, where bonds tend to be familial or even sacred" (p. 47). In organizations where this occurs, bureaucratic lines are blurred, and the need to manage people is reduced because people manage themselves in accordance with the shared vision. In the all-too-rare instances where this kind of fundamental change in structure occurs, organizations are truly transformed and become virtuous enterprises. According to Sergiovanni,

> When purpose, social contract, and local school autonomy become the basis of schooling, two important things happen. The school is transformed from an organization to a covenental community, and the basis of authority changes, from an emphasis on bureaucratic and psychological

authority to moral authority. To put it another way, the school changes from a secular organization to a sacred organization, from a mere instrument designed to achieve certain ends to a virtuous enterprise. (p. 102)

How did this one elementary school become such a special and caring place? I can assure you that it wasn't an accident, and it didn't happen overnight. It was a gradual change based on a simple idea that created a powerful vision that gave the school a unifying purpose: *No child shall fail!* Over the years, countless small and not-so-small decisions were made that enhanced that vision until it became not just an attractive idea, but a compelling reality.

The virtuous enterprises that schools—or other organizations, for that matter—can become are invariably structured in such a way that caring is reflected throughout the entire community. This is never an accident: Caring organizations are created by purposeful design. As Cashman (1998) has noted, a sense of purpose has a powerful transformational impact on organizations:

Nothing happens without purpose. A seed would never sprout. The planets in the heavens would not move in perfect symmetry. The laws of nature would cease to function. The artist would not paint. The musician would not play. The leader would not lead. Purpose gives meaning and direction to all of life. Without purpose we cease to be. . . . Because purpose is transformational, it converts average-performing organizations, families or relationships into highly effective ones. It transforms employees, spouses or friends into co-partners. With purpose managers become leaders. (pp. 66–68)

If one can accept the premise that building caring organizations is never an accident, but rather the result of purposeful design based on a collective vision, one must also come to the realization that the process of arriving at that collective vision is never easy. The principal of Zenia Elementary built that school's vision with his faculty and staff over a period of sixteen years.

By the way, I'm constantly amazed that people assume that the process of vision building is the responsibility and even the prerogative of the leader. Many people are absolutely convinced that the leader can and should craft a vision for the organization in her or his brain and then magically transfer that vision to everyone who is a part of the organization. And then, of course, they will all live happily ever after!

When I was interviewed for my last position as a dean at the University of La Verne, I was asked the following question by a member of the search committee: "What is your vision for the College of Education and Organizational

Leadership at the University of La Verne?" "Finally," I thought, "a question that doesn't require a great deal of thought on my part." I immediately replied, "I don't have one!" (By the way, in most instances, this is probably the wrong response if you want to be the successful candidate for a leadership position, since most people tend to believe that a leader should be—above all else—a visionary!) When pressed to justify why I didn't have the requisite vision at hand, I explained that it would be both presumptuous and foolish for me to assume that I could frame a vision for someone else, and beyond foolish to assume that I could pull a vision out of a hat for a whole organization full of people. However, I did assure the search committee that I felt very capable of working effectively with others over time to frame a vision for the College of Education and Organizational Leadership. Of course, I had a pretty good idea of what I thought a college like ours could and perhaps should be. But at the same time, I realized that it's simply not possible to arrive at a vision for an organization without embarking on a journey of discovery with all those who will be dramatically and fundamentally affected by that vision.

Zenia Elementary School was a virtuous enterprise where all the employees did, in fact, seem more like volunteers than employees. All of us who visited the school and witnessed the power of the shared vision were convinced that this was true. In all my years in educational leadership roles, I don't believe I've seen another school where all the teachers and other staff members refused to take sick days because they were convinced that their students and their colleagues needed them to be in school every single day. That kind of dedication is what we see from people who identify so much with the values of the workplace that they are more like volunteers than employees. De Pree (1989) says that the best people in organizations are more like volunteers than employees. Because they are like volunteers, these people "do not need contracts, they need covenants" (p. 28).

There could be more incredibly successful schools like Zenia Elementary if people cared enough to make it so. How about your school? Is it a virtuous enterprise? Have you and your colleagues come to the understanding that the most important thing in organizational life is deciding what's most important? Are the people who work in your school more like volunteers than employees? Do you and your colleagues have a shared vision for what your school or school district can be? Are your personal priorities in line with that vision? Do you accept your responsibility to act like a tall radio beacon beaming out a positive message in all directions, a message that will help to create a field of caring and concern for everyone in your organization?

TAKE TIME TO REFLECT

1. See if you can determine what the official vision statement is for your particular school or organization. Do you feel that the statement reflects an appropriate vision for your school or organization? If not, what changes or additions would be needed to make the vision statement more appropriate?

2. What kind of messages are people as tall radio beacons of information beaming out in your school or organization? What kind of messages are you beaming out in your interactions with others each day? What would have to happen in your school or organization to get all the messages from all the people on the same positive frequency?

CHAPTER EIGHTEEN

WHY DO I CHOOSE TO LEAD?

Clearly, serving as a leader (by now you should know that I believe teachers are among the very best leaders) is not all fun and games. While leadership clearly has its rewards, it also has its costs, and those costs can be substantial. In Chapter 10, where we explored what it means to be responsible, I shared several quotations from Heifetz and Linsky (2002). In their insightful book, *Leadership on the Line*, these authors described in detail some of the dangers of leading. They warned those who would lead that leaders frequently get booed rather than cheered, and that they may have to dodge tomatoes or even bullets. Furthermore, Heifetz and Linsky warned that leaders have to be willing to "stomach hostility," "take the heat," and even take casualties that are "almost too painful to endure"! Frankly the prospect of dodging tomatoes, much less bullets, doesn't sound all that appealing to me! There is a whole world of choices related to how one might earn a living, so why would any right-minded individual choose to follow a path that is fraught with tomatoes and bullets?

For five years, I lived next door to the world's greatest medical supplies salesperson. I kid you not—this guy was an incredible medical supplies salesperson! For seven out of eight years, he was recognized by his company with an award designating him as the national salesperson of the year. Because of his unique set of skills and talents coupled with his extraordinary performance, he was frequently offered promotions to management positions by his company, which he always politely declined. He declined the promotions because he loved what he was doing, and it showed—not just in the sales quotas he met and exceeded—but in the financial rewards that accrued to him, as well.

Because of his success, my neighbor, Jim, had to find places to put his money. He owned several other houses in our neighborhood that he rented, he owned shares in other real estate ventures, and he had a place at the lake. One year, Jim bought a lot on the golf course at Edisto Island, South Carolina, where he built a beautiful vacation home for his family. He purchased eight or nine cars while he was my neighbor. There were several BMWs along with a Cadillac, station wagons, and a few trucks mixed in for good measure. He owned three boats of various sizes that he selected for use in terms of the particular nautical activity he was planning. This guy was incredibly successful and he wasn't yet forty years of age!

Despite his business success, one could not be even the slightest bit jealous of Jim. In fact, those of us who knew him well were happy for his success because he was exactly the kind of person who deserved it. Not only was he a great salesperson, but he was also a terrific guy, a wonderful neighbor, father, husband, and friend. Jim was a great, big, old teddy bear of a man with a ready smile that was even wider than he was tall. He was also a sensitive, kind, and generous human being with the power to draw people to him like a magnet. (Maybe that's one reason he could sell all those medical supplies as well as he did.)

There were many terrific benefits that I enjoyed simply by being Jim's neighbor. For example, he frequently included me in the group that participated in his annual weeklong fishing excursion on the inland waterway near Beaufort, South Carolina. Jim also accorded me first refusal on his cast-off consumer goods when he decided to upgrade. I purchased a couple of used BMWs and a boat from Jim during the five years that I lived next door to him. All these benefits were wonderful, but maybe the best thing of all about being Jim's neighbor was that he and his lovely wife had three incredible little boys who were perfect playmates for my two elementary-school-age sons.

When it came to playing together, his boys and my boys fit together like the fingers of one hand interlaced with the fingers of the other. When we first moved there, the boys ranged in age from four to ten, enjoyed playing the same games, and seldom argued or fought with each other. My sons loved being over at Jim's house. In fact, during the summers they did just about everything but take their nightly baths and sleep over there. I kept telling myself that the main reason that all the kids played at Jim's house was because his children had all the latest toys and gadgets known to humankind, in addition to a well-stocked refrigerator. Jim's kids and their friends had access to a regulation pool table, a big-screen television and a VCR (way before these items became common-place in middle-class homes), and all the characters and paraphernalia ever invented for GI Joe, Masters of the Universe, and Star Wars as each, in turn, became popular with American youngsters.

One day, my oldest son, Patrick, who was about ten or eleven at the time, came home from a great day of fun, food, and frolic over at Jim's house. He walked into the house fairly beaming and declared, "You know what, Dad? If I could pick anybody in the world to be my father, it would be Jim!" To my credit, I laughed out loud as I replied, "Me, too, Patrick! Me, too!" More than twenty years have slipped by since my firstborn uttered these words to me, but I still occasionally remind him of what he said to me that day when I want to get his goat. What I never tell him is that there were times during his middle-to-late teenage years when his mother and I would have gladly traded him for almost any other kid in the neighborhood. Patrick's over-whelmingly positive response to Jim when he was a young child was cer-tainly understandable, and I'd like to think that, just like my wife and me, most other parents would gladly trade their offspring if given the opportunity at certain times during their children's developmental years.

The kind of success that Jim enjoyed can make a normal person question some of his or her life choices, especially in terms of career. Jim was incred-ibly successful and he made it look effortless. When I would leave home for work in the mornings, Jim's car would still be parked in his driveway. Most days, when I would return home from work, his car would already be parked in his driveway. During the summer, Jim would go on what he referred to as his "summer schedule." On his summer schedule, Jim would take off from work at noon on Thursday, pack up the kids and wife, and go to his vacation home at Edisto Island for a long weekend. It seemed to me that Jim could do this every single week during the summer if he chose to do so.

When I was younger, I occasionally questioned my choice of career. Once, in a period of extreme frustration while serving as a high school prin-cipal, I seriously thought about giving up my career as an educator and going back to law school. And if not a lawyer, then who knows? Maybe I could have been a movie star or, better yet, a country singer. Or perhaps I could have been a sports announcer, or maybe even an astronaut. Sometimes, I even think that I could have been a damn good medical supplies salesperson—maybe not as good as Jim, but certainly good enough to enjoy some of the financial rewards that he and his family enjoyed.

Fortunately, whenever I have felt this way, reality has always set in, and I have come to my senses. Jim once told me that he loved lying in his bed at night and contemplating all those people using his medical supplies. He said he got excited by the prospect of people consuming large amounts of his gauze, bandages, syringes, lap sponges, and the like. I promise you that he had a sincere look on his face when he told me these things, so I believe he was being absolutely truthful. Looking back, I'm convinced that Jim's great passion for his work was a big part of the reason he was such an incredible medical supplies salesperson and I would probably have been, at best, a pretty mediocre one. I would have been mediocre because, no matter how much they paid me, the thought of people consuming large quantities of my products would simply not be enough to sustain me on a daily basis. And while Jim made selling large quantities of medical supplies look easy, it wasn't. Doing what Jim did as well as he did it required a great deal of talent, commitment, and hard work.

But there's another far more important reason that I have devoted my working life to teaching and serving in other leadership roles instead of making my living in another way. Like most others who are serving or who have served in these roles, I want to feel that my life counts for something, that I make a difference each day when I go to work. I want to feel that my life has touched the lives of others in significant ways. When I look back over what I have accomplished in my life, I don't want to have to rely on the size of my bank balance to measure my worth as a human being. Like so many other professional educators I know, I want to feel that if I had never lived, the world would somehow be deprived of something valuable and important. Please don't misunderstand me: I don't mean this as a criticism of medical supply salespeople, because I have tremendous respect for what my friend Jim accomplished in a distinguished sales career. But I've often thought that if something were to happen to Jim, then someone else, although perhaps far less talented and committed, would step into the breach and deliver those medical supplies without losing a beat.

Professional educators are not like medical supply salespeople or astronauts or country singers. Teachers, counselors, principals, superintendents, and all the others in our profession help to shape the lives of others in ways so special and unique that every one of us is irreplaceable! That's an important part of why I am a professional educator and why I have chosen to serve in countless formal and informal leadership roles throughout most of my career. It's also the reason why I have never had a single day I didn't want to go to work, although I have to admit that there were some days on the job that I enjoyed a good deal less than others.

Whenever I think that perhaps I made the wrong career choice, I like to remember students like Charles, a seventh-grade nonreader whom I taught during my first year out of college. I want to remember just how much he needed me to help him learn to read and write so that he could learn what others had to teach him, how to express himself effectively, and eventually, how to be a fully functioning member of society. If I live to be one hundred years old, I'll never forget that last day of school when big, awkward Charles came up to me, shyly held out his hand, and opened it to reveal a shiny purple and silver fishing lure—his thank-you gift to me for the many hours of individual attention I had given him during the school year. It was his gift, not just for teaching him how to read and to write, but also for acknowledging and respecting his dignity as a human being.

That shiny purple and silver fishing lure is just about the best gift I have ever received from anyone. I must have caught more than one hundred large-mouth bass with it over the years. Although it's now too old and beat up to use anymore, I still have it in the top drawer of my fishing tackle box as a powerful reminder of just what it means to be a professional educator. That beautiful and totally unexpected gesture from Charles on the last day of school more than thirty-five years ago still brings me great satisfaction and pure joy whenever I think of it.

This chapter began with a description of some of the dangers of leadership as posed by Heifetz and Linsky (2002). Their vivid description of the downside of leadership provided the backdrop for the central question that was posed as the focus for the chapter: So why would any right-minded individual choose to follow a path (such as leadership or teaching) that is fraught with tomatoes and bullets? Since we let Heifetz and Linsky set up the key question to open this chapter for us, it's only fair that we should give them the opportunity to answer it, too. Besides, they have answered the question so beautifully:

> So the answer to the question "Why lead?" is both simple and profound. The sources of meaning in the human experience draw from our yearning for connection to other people. The exercise of leadership can give life meaning beyond the usual day-to-day stakes—approval of friends and peers, material gain, or the immediate gratification of success—because, as a practical art, leadership allows us to connect with others in a significant way. The word we use for that kind of connection is love. (p. 209)

So you see leaders are really not like medical supply salespeople, movie stars, astronauts, or country singers. People who serve as leaders are drawn to leadership roles because these roles provide them opportunities to connect with others in ways that are so fundamental that the effect on human lives can be quite profound and lasting. The more I reflect on it, the more I believe it is more appropriate to say that people are drawn to leadership roles more than that they consciously choose those roles. In fact, I would go so far as to say that leadership chooses people rather than the other way around. At least that's true for exceptional leaders. Margaret Wheatley (2005) has put it this way:

> Shall I say it again? I shall say it again. We [leaders] do what we are called to do because we are called to do it. We walk silently, willingly, down the well-trodden path still lit by the fire of millions. And the rest, I know now, is not our business. (p. 244)

TAKE TIME TO REFLECT

1. Have you ever thought about why are you presently serving in a leadership role or aspiring to be in a leadership role? In the words of Cashman (1998),

    Why [italics in original] is one of the most powerful words in our language. "Why?" is the question that calls us to meaning; it forces us to look beneath the surface into the deeper essence of things. "Why?" is the question that directs us onto the path of purpose. (p. 63)

    To use Cashman's word, what is your fundamental purpose for leading? What is it that brought you to this particular path of purpose?

2. What are some of the most significant costs of leadership to the leader and to her or his family? What are some of the most significant rewards? Are there practical ways that leaders can minimize the costs of leadership while enhancing the rewards, and still maintain a high level of integrity and effectiveness?

CHAPTER NINETEEN

WHAT DO LEADERS OWE TO THOSE WHO FOLLOW?

"What do leaders owe to those who follow?" Now there's an important question for anyone who aspires to a position of leadership! Are there any universally accepted standards to guide leadership behavior as leaders strive to meet their obligations to those who willingly give up the freedom to wander off in their own direction, and, instead, choose to go in the same direction as the group and the leader? If there are no universal standards, is there at least a reasonable set of guidelines that can help leaders meet their obligations to those whom they lead? By the way, the question, "What do leaders owe to those who follow?" is not to be confused with related, but slightly different, questions such as "What do followers want from their leaders?" or "What do leaders owe to their employers?" which I believe are also important questions that have decidedly different—if not always less complex—answers, depending on one's point of view.

Several years ago, on April 26, 2003, Warren Bennis visited our university and gave a spirited and entertaining presentation based on *Geeks and Geezers* (2002), an interesting and insightful book that he had written with Robert J. Thomas. This book examines the differences between generations of highly successful leaders at opposite ends of the age spectrum—those over the age of seventy and those under the age of thirty. At the end of his presentation, Bennis provided an opportunity for questions from his audience. I took this opportunity to ask the question that is the subject of this chapter, "What do leaders owe to those who follow?" I'm glad I asked, because I was absolutely delighted with his answer. Bennis thought for just a moment about my question and then said that he thought, first, that leaders owe followers the opportunity to be proud of the place where they work. The second thing he said that leaders owe to their followers is an opportunity to be acknowledged for the contributions they make to the organization. Finally, he said that leaders are obligated to remind followers about the things that are important.

I now know why Bennis has been an advisor to four presidents and is widely recognized as one of the foremost leadership and management gurus in the world. In his answer to my question, Bennis said a great deal in very few words. His response clearly reminds us that the things that leaders owe to their followers go well beyond the basic employment contract. In fact, I think it's pretty safe to say that leaders would not be leaders unless they fulfilled equally powerful unwritten contracts with their followers, who in turn give them permission to lead through their willingness to follow.

People desperately need to be able to be proud of the places where they work. After all, the majority of people spend a disproportionately large portion of their lives engaged in their work. Work is so important in the lives of most people that in many cases work almost becomes who they are and not just something they do to earn a living. If you recall the description of my Uncle Cecil as related in Chapter 4, he was, first and foremost, a carpenter by trade. After that, he was an intelligent, thoughtful, caring man. Cecil was also a Southerner, his views on everything including life, religion, and politics having been shaped by the culture and traditions of that region of the country. Furthermore, Cecil Yelvington was a husband, a brother, an uncle, a fisherman, a junk collector, a gardener, and a whole lot more—but first and always, he was a carpenter by trade. He was proud of what he did as a carpenter and even more proud of how well he did it.

So how can leaders provide their followers with the opportunity to be proud of what they do and the places where they work? Surely there is no magic formula to accomplish this goal since organizations are so different from each other, but there are some constants that translate from one organization to another. Perhaps the single most important thing that leaders can do to ensure that their followers develop feelings of pride in what they do and in the places where they work is to help them realize a sense of purpose in their work. Cashman (1998) has pointed out the importance of purpose to an organization: "Purpose releases energy. The higher the purpose, the greater the energy. Purpose also frees us. The more profound the purpose, the greater the sense of freedom. Purpose opens up possibilities" (p. 72).

Of course all organizations have a purpose, and they all stand for something. The problem is that many people have no idea what that purpose is or what their organizations stand for. Wheatley (2005) has proclaimed that "the organizations that people love to work in are those that have a sense of history, identity and purpose. Companies that have stood for something in the past, that stand for something now, provide compelling reasons for people to work hard" (p. 74). Leaders have the responsibility to ensure that the purpose for the existence of the organization, the central driving force behind all that happens in the organization, is made clear in documents such as mission or vision statements, and that the purpose is communicated to everyone in the organization over and over again.

In addition to communicating the purpose being served through work, leaders can also find better ways to effectively communicate the successes of the organization, even small successes, and provide opportunities for everyone who is a part of the organization to celebrate those successes. Finally, leaders can work with their fellow employees to help build organizations that are ethical and honest and respected in their particular industry for their values orientation. I'm reasonably sure that all of us would be proud to work in our organizations if those organizations were ethical and honest and widely respected for the way in which they do business!

Let's move now to Bennis's second point about acknowledging contributions in the workplace. How can leaders provide opportunities for their employees to be acknowledged for the contributions they make to the organization? As far as I am concerned, this is an easy one: Just do it! Leaders simply have to take the time and make the effort to let others in the organization know how much they respect and appreciate extraordinary contributions (and all good employees make lots of these) to the achievement of the mission of the organization. It's a certainty that people work for much more than a salary. They work for the joy of accomplishing a task, for the satisfaction of doing a job extremely well, and for the self-esteem that comes with the recognition that they have done a job extremely well.

There is an entire chapter in this book, Chapter 15, that is devoted to the importance of doing the little things well. Recognition of individual and group contributions to the organization is one of those "little things" that is really a "big thing," in that recognition for contribution frequently turns out to be the ultimate difference maker in how people feel about their work, their leaders, and even the organizations for which they work. I am convinced that showing appreciation for the contributions that people make to their organizations is one of those deciding factors that divides the winners from the losers in organizations and in life. Therefore, I devote a lot of my work time to writing notes and e-mailing expressions of appreciation and congratulations to my colleagues for a job well done. I take every opportunity I can find to publicly acknowledge significant contributions to our organization by others, and I am careful to always share the credit for our successes with all those who have played a role in those successes. In fact, in our organization we frequently celebrate successes in a public way so people's contributions to the organization can be acknowledged and appreciated as widely as possible.

Bennis's last point, that leaders have an obligation to remind people of what's important is, of course, a critical component of the debt that leaders owe to followers if they hope to promote a caring, moral climate in any organization. As Johnson (2005) has noted, "Leaders promoting integrity first define and then focus attention on central ethical values" (p. 252). It's easy for people in organizations to lose sight of what's important, given the constant swirl of job-related pressures in almost any workplace, not to mention the stresses placed on human beings by the many conflicting and demanding roles they play in their personal lives. Unless leaders frequently remind all those who are part of an organization about its mission, its vision, and its promise for the future—the basic values that define the organization—there is always the possibility, or even the likelihood, that these things will be lost in the shuffle. When this happens, organizations can become fragmented and even dysfunctional. Employees lose focus and spend valuable time and energy tilting at windmills rather than slaying dragons. As Welch (2005) has cautioned leaders,

> You have to talk about vision constantly—basically to the point of gagging. There are times I talked about the company's direction so many times in one day that I was completely sick of hearing it myself. But I realized the message was always new to someone. And so you keep on repeating it. And you talk to *everyone* [italics in original]. (p. 68)

If I could convince people in organizations to do just one thing, it would be to regularly talk about the things they value as an organization, for those are truly the things around which everything else should revolve.

Bennis has provided us a brief but very good list of the debts that leaders owe to those who follow. Certainly, there are any number of other possible candidates for this list. And although I don't believe an exhaustive list of all the possible debts that leaders owe to their followers is particularly necessary or even useful, there are a few other critical aspects of the unwritten contract between those who lead and those who follow that I want to acknowledge, because I believe they are helpful in better defining the true nature of the debt.

Near the top of any list of debts that leaders owe to those who follow is honesty. "That nearly 90 percent of constituents want their leaders to be honest above all else is a message that all leaders must take to heart" (Kouzes and Posner, 1995, p. 22). Honesty is a complex concept; it is far more than simply telling the truth about chopping down the cherry tree. Autry (1991) has hinted at the complexity of honesty:

> When I talk about honesty, I don't just mean honesty of words; I also mean honesty of feelings . . . honesty entails learning to see yourself as others see you and learning to openly and honestly express emotions in the context of the workplace. . . . Of all the faults I find with managers worldwide, the most common is the unwillingness, inability, or the fear of being honest with employees about performance, particularly negative performance. But you must be honest. It is the key to a productive workplace, and it is the key to avoiding gossip, rumors, and other destructive behaviors. Honesty involves giving employees information. Information is the single most nurturing element in any organization. Remember that nobody ever did a worse job from having too much information. (p. 48)

Honesty is a particularly critical leadership trait because it is the primary precondition for trust, and no one can lead without trust. How do leaders become worthy of trust? Kouzes and Posner (1999) have told us that "to become fully trusted, we must be open—to others but also with others. An open door is a physical demonstration of a willingness to let others in. So is an open heart. This means disclosing things about yourself" (p. 85). Furthermore, as Kouzes and Posner (1995) have pointed out, "It's clear that if we're to willingly follow someone—whether it be into battle or into the boardroom, into the classroom or into the back room, into the front office or to the front lines—we first want to assure ourselves that the person is worthy of our trust" (p. 22).

Bennis and Goldsmith (2003) have suggested that, "to build trust, we need environments where people feel free to voice dissent; where people are rewarded for disagreeing: where innovation and failure are tolerated" (p. 4). According to these writers, trusting environments are built by leaders who display four characteristics:

> First, the leader has competency. The foundation of leadership is built on the belief that the leader has the capacity to do the job. . . . Second, there must be congruity—the leader must be a person of integrity with values to match actions. . . . Third, people want a sense that the leader has constancy

and is on their side. . . . Finally, a leader is someone who is caring and trusted, who is genuinely concerned about the lives of the people served. (pp. 4–5)

One of the most discussed and written about debts of leadership has been described in terms of service and serving. Greenleaf (1977) was among the first to talk about leadership in this way. Greenleaf has even expressed the belief that serving is, in fact, the defining characteristic of outstanding leaders: "The great leader is seen as servant first, and that simple fact is the key to his greatness" (p. 7). Greenleaf further asserts that organizations can't bestow leadership on individuals, but that leadership can be granted only by those who agree to be led based on their perceptions of the ability and willingness of the leader to serve them:

A new moral principle is emerging which holds that the only authority deserving one's allegiance is that which is freely and knowingly granted by the led to the leader in response to, and in proportion to, the clearly evident servant stature of the leader. Those who choose to follow this principle will not casually accept the authority of existing institutions. *Rather, they will freely respond only to individuals who are chosen as leaders because they are proven and trusted as servants* [italics in original]. (p. 11)

Greenleaf isn't alone in his views of leadership. Blanchard and Hodges (2003), for example, have described servant leaders as those "who consider their position as being on loan and as an act of service" (p. 15). Bennis and Goldsmith (2003) have made it clear that leaders "do not stand above those who follow, but stand with them" (p. 5).

But how can a leader become a servant to his followers? De Pree (1989) offers many examples of how leaders can serve. He has said that leaders serve by "liberating people to do what is required of them in the most effective and humane way possible" (p. 1). Leaders serve in this sense by removing obstacles and granting freedom and space so that an organization's employees can do their jobs in a creative, elegant, and graceful manner. De Pree has said that leaders serve when they ask those whom they are serving for meaningful input and then respond to that input by acting appropriately. At its most fundamental level, serving implies taking care of others by seeking to discover and understand their needs and then striving to meet those needs in the best way possible.

Perhaps one of the more significant debts that leaders owe to those who follow is a sense of optimism—an abiding belief that things will improve—that there will be a brighter tomorrow with a happier and more productive life for all of those who share in the daily life of an organization. There are innumerable peaks and valleys in the lives of organizations just as there are ups and downs in the lives of the people who make up those organizations. During the darkest hours, a positive outlook from the leader, a declaration that there are solutions to problems, some small sign of unshakable confidence in the future, a simple smile in the face of adversity can lift people up and let them know that all is not lost. As Loehr and Schwartz (2003) have put it, "The mental energy that best serves full engagement is realistic optimism—seeing the world as it is, but always working positively towards a desired outcome or solution" (p. 108).

Optimistic leaders make us believe that Little Orphan Annie was right in her rousing and inspirational musical declaration, "The sun will come out tomorrow!" (Charnin 1977). Kouzes and Posner (1995) have reminded us that "it's part of the leader's job to show people that they can win" (p. 14). Furthermore, they have declared, "we expect our leaders to be enthusiastic, energetic, and positive about the future. We expect them to be inspiring—a bit of the cheerleader as a matter of fact" (p. 24). Csikszentmihalyi (2003) has echoed the importance of optimism to successful leadership in his description of outstanding business leaders who combined high achievement with strong moral commitment, "Perhaps the most obvious trait one notices in these leaders is what one of them characterized as 'pathological *optimism*'"[italics in original] (p. 156). Leaders owe a great deal to those who follow, but perhaps above all else, leaders owe them a strong sense of hope.

From the preceding discussion, one could conclude that leaders owe much to those who follow. While a leader's debts to his or her followers are many and varied, it has been suggested in this chapter that several stand above others in terms of their importance. Among the chief debts that leaders owe to those who follow are the opportunity to be proud of the place where they work, the chance to be acknowledged for their contributions to the organization, and the opportunity to be reminded of what is most important in the life of the organization. Leaders also owe followers honesty so that an atmosphere of openness and trust can evolve and flourish in the organization. Leaders are responsible—not just for leading in a classic sense, but also for caring for and serving those who follow. Finally, the last significant debt of the leader as discussed in this chapter is to radiate hope and optimism for the future of the organization and for those who spend a great portion of their lives living and working in the organization.

Of course, this brief discussion of the debts of leadership barely scratches the surface of all that leaders owe to their followers. Clearly, every human being in an organization, from the chief executive officer to the person who cuts the grass and rakes the leaves, deserves dignity, purpose, meaning, recognition, and a sense of satisfaction in exchange for the commitment, effort, and energy that he or she expends on behalf of the organization. Great leaders ensure that all these debts and more are paid in full.

In November 2004, I had the opportunity to visit with Margaret Wheatley—the well-known writer, thinker, and lecturer in the area of leadership—during a reception that was held in her honor. I really wanted to get her best thoughts about what she regarded as the debts that leaders owe to their followers, so I prefaced the question, "What do leaders owe to those who follow?" by telling her that I would give her some time to think about my question and then ask for her answer later in the evening. As soon as she heard the question, Wheatley came back with a question for me. "Can I answer your question right now?" "Sure go ahead," I answered. Her response was simple, but oh, so elegant. "How about everything! Leadership is a gift to the leader from those who follow because leadership is a relationship—not a title" (Personal communication, November 30, 2004).

TAKE TIME TO REFLECT

1. Every significant role that one plays in life has certain debts and rewards that simply go with the territory. For example, there are rewards associated with parenthood, but our children always find ways to remind us that there are a number of debts, as well. Marriage has debts and rewards, and so does friendship. This chapter has been devoted to a discussion of some of the debts of leadership, those things that leaders owe to those who follow. What do you believe are some of the other important things that leaders owe to those who follow? What do you think are the things that leaders have a right to expect from their followers in exchange for their leadership?

2. What evidence do you have that you have been paying your debts to those whom you are serving in a leadership role? Are you providing an opportunity for them to be proud of the place where they work or to be recognized for the contributions they make to the organization, and so forth? In what ways are you accomplishing these things?

CHAPTER TWENTY

CAN I CARE ENOUGH TO BE MY OWN BEST FRIEND?

"Can I care enough to be my own best friend?" probably sounds like a ridiculous question to most people, especially to leaders, but I can assure you that it's not. We frequently hear people say, "You know, he's his own worst enemy." But we never hear them say, "You know, she's her own best friend." I wish that we would hear this! Of all the friends we can ever have in our lives, none is so important as the friend that we can be to ourselves. A primary life task for anyone, but especially for leaders, is to develop a close and supportive friendship with oneself, a friendship so supportive and caring that it could even be termed a loving relationship. The nature and strength of the relationships that we are able to build with ourselves are absolutely critical for leaders because we can give away to others only those things that we already possess. If we don't have an abundance of self-love and caring, then we don't have any caring and love left over that we can give away to others. A leader who lacks the capacity to give away love and caring to others is seriously handicapped!

Most of us have grown up in a highly competitive culture where criticism is much more common than praise, where the world is divided into winners and losers based on some rather ridiculous criteria. For example, isn't it absurd that the silver medal winner in an Olympic competition is regarded by many as a failure? Isn't it bizarre that the human being who produces the second-best performance in the entire world in a particular sports event can be tagged with the label "loser"? Unfortunately, it's a sad but accurate commentary on the overly competitive society in which we live.

Because of the competitive nature of our society and the way in which we have been schooled never to be satisfied with anything less than total victory, many of us have internalized a personal style that embraces a preference for criticism rather than praise. We are constantly focusing on what's wrong with us and never on what's right. Because we have been encouraged by our parents, mentors, and teachers from a very early age to push ourselves to the next highest level and never to be satisfied with second best, we have in turn learned to drive those around us to also drive themselves.

In American society, the cultural norm is that we must all run faster, jump higher, compile a higher grade point average, be prettier or more handsome, drive a more expensive car, live in a bigger house, make more money, and so forth than anyone around us. Unfortunately, there can only be one Number 1 in any category, and sadly, most of us have been made to feel from a very early age that we must strive to be Number 1 in every category. Loehr and Schwartz (2003) have painted a vivid picture of just how hectic life has become in our highly competitive, digital age:

> Our rhythms are rushed, rapid fire and relentless, our days carved up into bits and bytes. We celebrate breadth rather than depth, quick reaction rather than considered reflection. We skim across the surface, alighting for brief moments at dozens of destinations but rarely remaining for long at any one. We race through our lives without pausing to consider who we really want to be or where we really want to go. We're wired up, but we're melting down. (p. 3)

We live at warp speed with lofty standards imposed to measure success, so is it any wonder that most of us spend a good deal of our lives feeling like failures and causing others around us to feel like failures as well? Even in those instances where we do achieve momentary success, we can't rest on our laurels and enjoy the moment because fame is fleeting and we must continue to scramble for that next rung on all the ladders that we are climbing simultaneously. I am convinced that the constant drive to measure up to such demanding external standards has led us to internalize a preference for self-criticism.

If you don't believe that people tend to criticize themselves, then just listen to how you talk to yourself. How often do you criticize yourself both publicly and privately for your real and imagined shortcomings? When people give you compliments, how often do you deflect the kind words by denying the substance of what these people are saying? How many times have you told yourself that you're stupid or dumb, that you're "not okay"? If you had to give a speech to a group of people and tell them about your bad points, would that be easier for you than it would be to stand up in front of that same group and tell them about your good points? Typically, it is far easier and socially more acceptable for us to acknowledge our weaknesses than it is to acknowledge our strengths.

If most of us were to monitor our self-talk for just a short time, we might be surprised at how mean and unsympathetic we act toward ourselves. It's a pretty safe bet that you would never say to your best friend some of the things that you say to yourself. For example, if you were playing doubles tennis with your best friend, you would never say to him or her some of mean and ugly things that you probably say to yourself. If your friend were to double-fault while serving or were to miss an easy put-away shot, you wouldn't yell at your friend and call him or her a "bonehead," a "clumsy idiot," or a "stupid jerk." On the contrary, you would probably reach out and give your friend a nice friendly pat on the back to comfort him or her. You would tell your friend, "Look, it's okay. Don't worry about it. You'll do better next time!"

But if you are the one to make the error, then you might behave quite differently toward yourself than you would toward a friend. You might yell at yourself, throw your racquet to the ground in disgust, admonish yourself to "get your act together," tell yourself that "you are a terrible tennis player," and verbally kick yourself over and over again for your failure to measure up and execute the play properly. I know that I've seen lots of people do and say these kinds of things on tennis courts, racquetball courts, and golf courses.

The fact is that many of us say things to ourselves that we would never say to a best friend and treat ourselves in ways that we would never treat another person whom we care about . If we were to treat our best friends the way we treat ourselves in the little tennis scenario above, then most of us wouldn't have our best friends for very long! And if you treat yourself in such an abusive way, then I can promise you that you won't be much of a friend to yourself either.

I believe that the way we talk to ourselves greatly influences our self-concepts and significantly affects our capacity to be supportive and caring toward others as well. As Cashman (1998) has noted, "No one else can validate your value. It is for you to give yourself. Leaders can effectively validate and support others only if they have validated themselves first" (p. 61). Put another way, Cashman is simply telling us that leaders can give away to others only what they already have themselves. If we constantly focus our attention on our shortcomings and our failures, then we won't like ourselves very much. If we magnify our faults and tell ourselves that we are "not okay," then that is precisely what we will come to believe. And if leaders think poorly of themselves, then how can they hope to behave in supportive and caring ways toward others?

We all need to learn how to provide for ourselves the same kind of support and encouragement we so willingly and generously provide for our best friends. We must raise our awareness of the relationship that we have with ourselves and strive to improve that relationship by treating ourselves as we do our most special and highly valued friends. Every leader is bound to make mistakes. We must pay attention to our self-talk, and in those instances where we genuinely believe that we have made mistakes and a reprimand is in order, then we need to deliver that admonition in the same way as we would for our best friend.

As Bennis (1992) has reminded us, "They [leaders] not only believe in the necessity of mistakes, they see them as virtually synonymous with growth and progress" (p. 96). He notes that if you haven't failed, then you haven't tried very hard, and that "everywhere you trip is where treasure lies" (p. 149). Furthermore, Bennis cautions that "true learning must often be preceded by unlearning, because we are taught by our parents, our teachers, and friends how to go along, to measure up to their standards, rather than allowed to be ourselves" (p. 63). He reminds us that "by examining and understanding the past, we can move into the future unencumbered by it. We become free to express ourselves, rather than endlessly trying to prove ourselves" (p. 79).

Clearly, leaders mustn't be encumbered by the need to constantly prove themselves to others or, for that matter, the need to prove themselves to themselves either. Although we rightfully expect that leaders will make mistakes from time to time and that they will acknowledge those mistakes when it is appropriate to do so, it isn't necessary for leaders to be overly critical of themselves and to beat themselves up for their failures. In my experience, I have found that there is always an abundance of people out there who are willing and able to take on that particular responsibility for the leader.

Leadership requires the freedom to express caring for oneself as well as for others. Following are some suggested ways that leaders can exercise appropriate caring for themselves, and, in doing so, if they are fortunate, they may even become their own best friends:

1. *Always talk to yourself and treat yourself as you would a dear friend.* Be kind! Be understanding! Be gentle! Be patient! Make sure that, if you must criticize yourself, you do so with caring and concern. Remember,

if you can't count on yourself to be on your side when things are difficult, then on whom can you count?

2. *Learn how to play—not simply to win, but just to play.* If ultimate victory is the object of playing, then the joy of play cannot be fully appreciated. Relax and know that you don't have to prove anything to anyone when you are at play.

3. *Recognize your strengths, focus more on those strengths, and build from those strengths.* Never underestimate your strengths or overestimate your weaknesses. We are all better at some things than we are at others. We need to appreciate our good points more and abandon the self-defeating drive to be the best at everything all the time.

4. *Celebrate and enjoy your successes (even small successes) just as you would the successes of others about whom you genuinely care.* When you accomplish a goal that is important to you, reward yourself by saying nice things to yourself, sending yourself flowers, taking yourself out to dinner at a nice restaurant, giving yourself a day off from work, or buying yourself a new tie or a new purse. Pat yourself on the back and remind yourself that you are indeed a special person who has earned and deserves this good treatment.

5. *Seek to maintain a state of balance between your need to be productive in your professional life and your need to be satisfied in your personal life.* Remember that meaningful relationships are to be prized over plaques on the wall. To consistently perform at a high level and to be at their most effective, leaders must lead full and balanced lives.

6. *Strive to keep things in perspective.* It's easy to let small problems grow out of proportion and to imagine that they are much more serious than they really are. When you feel unduly stressed by a problem at work, try to measure it against something that is really important in your life, such as the health of your children or your spouse, or perhaps the loss of a special relationship that you hold dear. I frequently use this technique and I can promise you that, in most cases, your workplace problems seem far less important when they are put in perspective.

7. *Make it a habit to laugh every day.* When we laugh, we are giving ourselves the gift of joy. What better gift could we give to our best friend?

8. *Make sure you have someone you can talk with frankly and honestly when the need arises.* Leadership can be a lonely proposition at times.

In many situations, leaders cannot share their innermost feelings with others in the workplace—sometimes, not even with family. I have a friend who is a minister and he has a "contract friend" for just such occasions. He and his contract friend meet every now and then for lunch to talk about the things that are bothering each of them. They are not professional colleagues, nor are they social friends. Their one connection in life is to meet occasionally, listen carefully to the other's concerns, and give unbiased and honest feedback.

9. *Realize that the daily act of caring is extremely demanding and energy-consuming work.* No one person has the capacity to love and care for himself or herself and everyone else in the organization all the time without a great deal of support from others. Seek to build a climate of caring in the workplace, where others develop an appreciation and a willingness not just to care, but also to express that caring freely.

10. *Remember you* are not *the leadership role that you are playing.* A leader is only one of many aspects of who you are as a person. There are many other aspects of your humanity that are just as important, and some that are clearly more important than your role as a leader. Heifetz and Linsky (2002) have warned leaders about the danger they face when "colleagues, subordinates, and bosses treat you as if the role you play is the essence of you, the real you" (p. 188), and caution leaders not to "underestimate the challenge of distinguishing role from self" (p. 190). Heifetz and Linsky encourage leaders to "remember, when you lead, people don't love or hate you. Mostly they don't even know you. They love or hate the positions you represent" (p. 198).

11. *Embrace the notion that things are going to go awry in every organization no matter who occupies the leadership roles.* Leaders must accept this reality and realize that dealing with crises goes with the territory. As Welch (2005) has noted,

> Look, crises happen. As long as companies are made up of human beings, there will be mistakes, controversies, and blowups. There will be accidents, theft, and fraud. The cold truth is that some degree of unwanted and unacceptable behavior is inevitable. If people always followed the rules, there would be no police forces, courthouses, or jails. (p. 147)

12. *Enjoy the journey and forget about the destination.* Your life will be much more productive and much less stressful if you can learn to enjoy the journey. Remember, one never really arrives at that destination called perfection. Just relax: We are all merely on our way "to visit Bob."

Caring enough to become your own best friend should be a primary life goal for anyone who aspires to a leadership role. Through accepting, loving, and caring for yourself appropriately, you will discover that you possess a much greater capacity to accept, care for, and even come to love others with whom you live and work. If you can see the best in yourself, then you can also see and bring out the best in others. If we truly care enough to lead, then each of us in our own way must also care enough to become our own best friend. If leaders can master the art of becoming their own best friends, then perhaps they will achieve that state of being that Heifetz and Linsky (2002) refer to as a "sacred heart" and fulfill their purposes as leaders:

> The most difficult work of leadership involves learning to experience distress without numbing yourself. The virtue of a sacred heart lies in the courage to maintain your innocence and wonder, your doubt and curiosity, and your compassion and love even through your darkest, most difficult moments. . . . A sacred heart means you may feel tortured and betrayed, powerless and hopeless, and yet stay open. It's the capacity to encompass the entire range of human experience without hardening or closing yourself. It means that even in the midst of disappointment and defeat, you remain connected to people and to the sources of your most profound purposes. (p. 227)

TAKE TIME TO REFLECT

1. Are you your own best friend? How do you know? Can you cite some specific examples of how you have incorporated into your own life some of the suggestions on becoming your own best friend that are discussed above? Are there other steps you might take to become a better friend to yourself so that you might serve others better?

2. Write a letter to yourself describing your good points as a human being and as a leader. Don't be overly modest in completing this assignment. Give yourself the credit you deserve. Remember, if you don't recognize your finer points, then how can you expect others to do so?

CHAPTER TWENTY-ONE

WILL THAT BE A SENIOR
CUP OF COFFEE?

I t was almost ten years ago that I enjoyed my first senior cup of coffee. In case this hasn't yet happened to you, I can assure you that the initial senior cup of coffee is a significant milestone in anyone's life. The feeling one derives from this experience is equivalent to, but at the same time quite different from, that celebratory beer consumed by a twenty-one-year-old. My first senior cup of coffee was a genuine rite of passage!

My official move into old age happened something like this: I arrived early to a scheduled meeting on a consulting job and decided to reward myself for my punctuality by stopping by a fast-food restaurant for a steaming hot cup of coffee. As I approached the service counter at the restaurant, I was greeted by a friendly young woman who politely asked, "May I help you?"

"Yes," I replied. "Give me a cup of coffee."

"Senior?" she asked.

"I just want a regular cup of coffee," I said, not understanding her question.

"Will that be a senior coffee?" she persisted.

"What's a senior coffee?" I asked, with what must have been a puzzled look on my face.

"Thirty-five cents," the young woman answered with a laugh.

"Good! Then gimme a senior cup of coffee!" I said.

I don't know how I got old enough to qualify for a senior cup of coffee without realizing it, but somehow I did. Maybe it's a simple case of denial. It's not that I have a problem facing up to old age—it's just that I don't fully comprehend all the implications of my advancing years. Heck! I still write "brown" in the spot reserved for hair color on my driver's license application, and I haven't had brown hair for as long as anyone around me can remember. But I'm loyal like that. I refuse to forsake the brown hair that I was born with for the gray hair that apparently snuck up and replaced it one night while I was sleeping.

Although I am not particularly pleased with some aspects of aging such as joint pain and high blood pressure, there are a lot of good things about being older. For example, you don't have to worry about looking great in your clothes or even if your socks match. Your kids eventually grow up and have lives of their own. Most of us become more comfortable in our professional lives as we realize we don't have to climb mountains for other people—we can pick our own mountains! At some point, we older people can even begin to feel good about the size of our house payments compared to those of our younger neighbors.

There are all these things to feel good about and a whole lot more. Maybe one of the best things about growing older is both the opportunity and the inclination to become more reflective in our lives. For many of us, maturity brings with it a whole new perspective on where we've been and where we're headed, and leads us to question a lot of important choices already made or waiting to be made. This chapter focuses on some of the important questions that we should be asking ourselves, both as individuals and as leaders, as we strive to become more like the human beings and the leaders that we want to be.

Where am I on my life's journey as a human being and a leader? What have been the results of my thoughts, deeds, and actions on others who have trusted me to serve them in a leadership role? What are the things that I have done well—the things that I can feel good about? What are the things that I have done poorly—the things that I wish I had done differently? And perhaps most important, how can I use my successes and my failures to help me become a better person and a more faithful servant to those who have trusted me enough to allow me to lead? These are important questions that we should all be asking ourselves.

I am convinced that one of the critical qualities differentiating those who are truly leaders from those who would be leaders is a personal commitment to reflect continuously on the results of their thoughts, deeds, and actions on the lives of others and on the organizations that they serve. I believe this to be true because personal reflection is the unmistakable mark of the kind of genuine caring and commitment required on the part of all authentic leaders.

A leader's willingness to struggle with the results of decisions made, to question whether or not there may have been a better path than the one chosen, to suffer mightily and even to agonize at times alongside those adversely affected by the consequences of poor decisions—these are all part and parcel of caring leadership. The kind of personal reflection that I'm talking about allows leaders to grow from their mistakes and become better and more faithful servants to those who choose to follow. Experience without reflection is meaningless because thoughtful consideration of actions taken and the consequences resulting from those actions is how we are able to grow as leaders. I know many so-called experienced leaders who, rather than having twenty-five years of experience, have one year of experience twenty-five times. That is what happens to leaders who act and react without reflecting on their actions.

In his perceptive book, *Leadership Without Easy Answers* (1994), Heifetz points out what so many of us instinctively know but frequently forget: "Leadership is both active and reflective. One has to alternate between participating and observing" (p. 252). Unfortunately, many of us in leadership roles often get so caught up in actively participating in the chaotic swirl of events surrounding us that we forget all about our responsibility to also be thoughtful observers. As Loehr and Schwartz (2003) have warned,

> The consequence of living our lives at warp speed is that we rarely take the time to reflect on what we value most deeply or to keep these priorities front and center. Most of us spend more time reacting to immediate crises and responding to the expectations of others than we do making considered choices guided by a clear sense of what matters most. (p. 15)

If those entrusted with leadership roles "spend more time reacting to crises and responding to the expectations of others than they do making considered choices," they can never really lead effectively, because they will never be able to grasp the big picture that is paramount to gaining a clear understanding of what matters most.

Heifetz (1994) has illustrated this point with a wonderful analogy of someone who dances on a dance floor, as opposed to someone who watches others dancing from the vantage point of a balcony. Because of the activity and the focus required while actually dancing, a dancer is unable to be an effective observer of the entire dance. The dancer is certainly aware of the music and the person he or she is dancing with, and perhaps some of the other dancers in the immediate vicinity. But the observer from her or his vantage point on the balcony can see so much more because the observer has a bird's eye view of everything: the big picture, so to speak. The observer can see the orchestra performing, note who is dancing with whom and who is sitting out, and check out the people chatting at the refreshment table. The observer may even observe someone spiking the punch or a young man stealing a kiss from his best girl over in a dark corner.

The point is, of course, that the dance is so much more complex than it appears from the limited perspective of a single dancer. If one wants to really appreciate and understand that complexity of the dance, then it becomes necessary to periodically go up on the balcony and watch the dance from there. This is equally as true of leadership as it is of dancing. Leaders must occasionally go up on the balcony if they want to see the big picture. Leaders must periodically step back and reflect as thoughtful observers so that they can then act in ways that are in tune and consistent with the complexity of the dance that we know as leadership.

Heifetz (1994) suggests that "the right questions can help one get far enough above the fray to see the key patterns" (p. 253). Of course, I share the view that questions are a great way for leaders to get up on the balcony. That's why this entire book is about asking the right questions. Who knows? The right questions might even allow one to venture down into the basement and observe from time to time, which is perhaps just as important as observing from a vantage point above the fray.

Because I believe that reflection is so crucial to leadership, I frequently ask my students and workshop participants to do an assignment that causes them to reflect on their own thoughts, actions, and deeds in leadership roles. The assignment involves writing an honest and forthright letter to themselves in which they critique their thoughts, feelings, and actions as leaders. Some of the key questions that have provided the structure for this book are the questions I ask them to address in their letters.

Many, if not most, people find this to be a difficult assignment. It's difficult because we are not accustomed to reflecting: we are much more comfortable with acting and reacting. Most leaders are so busy trying to deal with the daily stresses and strains of leadership, in some cases just trying to survive, that they have never devoted the time and energy needed to analyze the positive and negative consequences of their actions as leaders or to evaluate whether or not they are on paths that will allow them to become the kind of human beings and leaders they would ultimately like to become.

As a conclusion to these very personal letters, I ask my students and workshop participants to make a commitment to do some tangible things to improve themselves as human beings and as leaders. I ask them to describe in detail those things they are committed to doing in the days and weeks and months ahead and to attach time lines so that something will actually happen and they will move themselves in the directions they wish to go.

When my students and workshop participants have finished their letters, I have them seal them in envelopes, address the envelopes to themselves, and give them to a close friend. They are told to instruct their friends to mail the letters to them at some time in the future when the friend feels that they may need a little boost to get back on track and strive harder to realize the promises they have made to themselves.

I have done this particular exercise on a number of occasions myself. Invariably, I am surprised at what it reveals to me. Occasionally, when I ask myself the question, "What do I care about?" I find that the answer is not the answer I want it to be for me. Maybe I find myself caring about things that are small and inconsequential in the big scheme of things. Although I hate to admit it, I may find myself caring about personal recognition or personal comfort. Or perhaps when I ask myself the question, "Why am I doing this?" I don't like the answer because I learn that my actions could be motivated by a desire to exercise personal power over others or to show off my superior knowledge or skill in a particular area rather than to help someone grow more competent in meeting his or her responsibilities.

Although I may not like the answers I receive when I ask myself these questions, it is critical that I ask them if I expect to become more like the person and the leader that I ultimately want to become. I have always believed that if a person genuinely cares about others, then that person will tell them the things that they *need* to hear rather than the things they *want* to hear. Without honest and accurate feedback to guide our future actions, how can we expect to continue to grow and develop and, ultimately, become more like the person we want to be? If we can care enough about others to tell them the things they need to hear, can we honestly be satisfied with doing anything less for ourselves? I don't think that we can. Do you?

I am at a point on my personal life's journey where I am continually struggling to make major decisions in both my professional and personal lives. Seven years ago, I made a decision to leave the University of South Carolina, where I had been a member of the faculty for more than twenty years, and move to another setting where the goals of the organization were more in tune with my own. Clearly, the goals of the University of South Carolina were not the same goals that attracted me to the institution more than twenty years before, and I needed to make a change if I wanted to be the best person I could be. I have now been in my present environment for seven years and have enjoyed it immensely, but the time is approaching for me to move on, and I will soon be retiring and going on to other things.

Maybe I can now become a country singer as I've always wanted to be, or to pen the great American novel that we all secretly wish that we could write. Maybe one day very soon I will spend most of my free time working as a volunteer so I can be certain that I am doing the things that I am doing because I am convinced that they need to be done, rather than because I get paid to do them. Whatever the decisions about how I spend my time might be, I know that we all have only a limited amount of time to make these kinds of decisions. Otherwise, external circumstances will surely make these decisions for us.

Many important changes are also taking place in my personal life. What will be the effect of these changes in the years ahead? At long last, my children are grown men. For better or for worse, I have done the parenting thing about as long and as well as I can do it. My relationship with my children will continue to evolve—it will never again be what it was. How will I relate to my children in the years ahead? Can I find the strength and understanding to let them be the people they choose to be rather than the people I would have them be? At long last, I have come to realize that I have no control over their lives, but then it is always an illusion to believe that we have control over the lives of others.

What about my relationship with the beautiful, caring, and talented woman I have been married to for almost forty years? What will be the direction of our relationship? Will each one of us have the will and the personal resources required to continue to reshape and revitalize the relationship in such a way that it will not only endure, but also will be more satisfying and rewarding than it has ever been before? I admit I don't know the answer to any of these questions. But I'm pretty sure that these are some of the questions that I ought to be asking myself about my personal and professional lives at this precise moment.

At the same time that all these critical questions are swirling in my mind, I find myself realizing that the answers that have worked for me in the past may not be the answers that will work for me in the future. Although I may not have definitive answers for my questions, there is one thing that I do know for sure: I haven't yet done enough in my life in a number of areas. I have not done enough as a friend, a colleague, a teacher, or a leader. I have not yet done enough as a father or a husband or a citizen of the world. I'm not unduly troubled by this realization, because it helps to reassure me that I will have plenty of important work to do in the years that remain. I believe that I have the potential to be a better person than I am today. I believe that we all do. But positive change is never easy. If any of us hopes to change anything for the better (and that's what leadership is all about), then several events must take place.

First, we must become aware of the nature of the problems that we are facing. We can't hope to solve problems if we aren't even aware that they exist. If we want things to be better than they are, then we have to make ourselves aware of the essential problems in our organizations and in our lives. As this book suggests, we must constantly question the status quo to accomplish this purpose. After all, that's essentially what reflection is all about.

The second event that must occur to make positive change happen is that we must genuinely want things to be different. Many people are perfectly satisfied with the status quo. They are either very comfortable and secure and happy with the way things are, or they are equally afraid of what they might become if they risk change. Significant change never occurs in an environment where people are satisfied with the status quo or are afraid to risk the present, no matter how undesirable it might be, for the promise of a better future. How can change occur when people refuse to embrace it?

The third and perhaps the most essential ingredient necessary for positive change to occur is a willingness to make personal sacrifices. People have to be willing to give up something—to sacrifice some of their comfort, their time, their energy, and perhaps even some of their legitimate power in order for positive change to occur. Change almost always carries significant costs, but it also usually offers great rewards.

Finally, there must be a realization that change is difficult. Successful change requires commitment, persistence, and a large measure of faith that there can be a better future. Significant change doesn't happen easily, and it doesn't occur overnight. As people dedicated to making a difference in the lives of others, leaders must believe that where they've come from as a person or as an organization or where they are at present isn't nearly as important as where they're headed.

I believe that organizations are, in fact, living systems and that organizational life, just like human life, is a journey. Where we go as organizations and as individuals is up to us. Wheatley (2005) has expressed a similar view:

> These days, a different ideal for organizations is surfacing. We want organizations to be adaptive, flexible, self-renewing, resilient, learning, intelligent—attributes found only in living systems. . . . Organizations are living systems. All living systems have the capacity to self-organize, to sustain themselves and move toward greater complexity and order as needed. They can respond intelligently to the need for change. (pp. 32–33)

Intelligent response to the need for change, both in individuals and in organizations, is the direct result of thoughtful, disciplined reflection that is based largely on asking the right questions. Leaders need always to be asking themselves, "What is possible for me and for all the others in this organization?" Leaders need to be eternally searching for the answers to questions such as "What do I stand for?" "What do *we* stand for?" "What can I be?" "What must I be?" "What can we be?" "What must we be?"

Through the years, I have been fortunate to have had numerous opportunities to travel around the country and occasionally around the world to interact with others serving in various formal and informal leadership roles. Although I believe that leaders everywhere are struggling with the same kinds of problems and issues, the ways in which they approach those problems and issues are as varied as the surroundings and circumstances in which these leaders may find themselves. At this point in my life, I am convinced that there are no pat answers that anyone can offer leaders to help make their tasks more manageable or that will help to lighten the burdens of leadership that weigh heavily on their shoulders.

Although I am forced to acknowledge that there are no pat answers, I am at the same time heartened by my belief that there are vast constellations of important questions that leaders can rely on to help them find their way in even the most uncertain of times and circumstances. Just as a bright star radiating its brilliance across thousands of light-years of time and space can provide guidance to a sailor lost in a vast sea, key questions such as "What do I care about?" "What do I believe about people?" and "Why am I doing this?" can help point the way for leaders struggling to fulfill the sacred promises they have to serve those who have trusted them enough to allow them to lead. It is indeed far better to know some of the questions than all of the answers! Although answers come and go like the changing of the seasons, the most critical questions remain eternal and serve as faithful beacons for leaders with the commitment and the courage to ask them.

TAKE TIME TO REFLECT

1. If we as leaders and human beings have some measure of immortality in this life, it is manifested in the impact that we have on the lives of others. Our immortality is measured in the lives we are privileged to touch and to change in positive ways as we carry out our duties and responsibilities as professionals, friends, family members, and so forth. Suppose for a moment that for some reason you are no longer a part of the organization where you are currently employed, or suppose that you are no longer there as a spouse or a parent or in some other role that is important in your life. Imagine that in five years you could come back and listen, unseen, while others talk about you in terms of what you meant to the organization or the family or to whatever entity you are imagining. What would you want to hear people say about you?

2. What are you doing to build your legacy as a leader? What are you willing to do? Write a letter to yourself outlining several steps you plan to take during the next few months to a year to move yourself toward becoming the kind of leader you ultimately want to become. There are a number of suggestions that you may want to adapt for this purposes included in the final chapter of this book. Pull out your letter periodically and check on your progress. Share your aspirations and results with another person who has a similar commitment to improve his or her leadership capabilities.

CHAPTER TWENTY-TWO

YOUR LEADERSHIP BECOMES YOU!

I was fifteen years old when I finally realized that I was never going to play center field for the Brooklyn Dodgers. This realization came to me rather suddenly and was the result of making three errors in the field during the first two innings of my inaugural high school varsity baseball game. The reality was that I didn't have the talent required to become a big-league baseball player. Wanting to be a professional baseball player just wasn't enough. So, like it or not, I was going to have to set my sights on being something else besides a sports hero.

Coming to the conclusion that I was never going to replace my hero, Duke Snider, as the center fielder for the Dodgers was painful. Like a lot of other young boys growing up in the 1950s and 1960s, sports were the most important thing in the world to me. Athletics were a big part of my life, and ballplayers were my chosen role models. Because I strongly identified with professional athletes, I wanted to be just like them in every way possible. I tried to walk like they walked, dress like they dressed, and talk like they talked. I would have loved to have gone around town with a big chaw of chewing tobacco tucked smugly in my cheek, but I was fairly certain that my mother would have killed me if I'd tried that.

Walking and dressing and talking and even chewing tobacco like big leaguers would never be enough to make me a professional baseball player. Being a professional baseball player also requires a high degree of speed, agility, strength, and coordination. These things I wasn't able to mimic, and therefore I couldn't realize this particular dream. Fortunately or unfortunately, my desire to chew tobacco and imitate the lives of big-league ballplayers ceased with the three errors. From that day forward, my life went in a different direction.

My attempts to mimic the lives of those who were my role models were not unique to me. All my friends did it in one way or another. Although a lot of them wanted to become professional athletes, some wanted to become the next Elvis, while still others wanted to become doctors, lawyers, or Indian chiefs. The point is that we all wanted to be something when we grew up, and we lived our lives for the most part in the ways we thought we needed to live them to reach our goals, no matter how ridiculous or unreachable those goals might have been. By the way, when I attended my thirty-fifth high school reunion several years ago, I discovered that, although our class hadn't produced any professional athletes, a number of my classmates had achieved a good many of their childhood dreams in one way or another.

How do we achieve our dreams? How do we learn to do something that we want to do or to become something that we want to be in life? How do human beings gain the knowledge and skills and attitudes necessary to function in the various roles they are required to fill to live full and productive lives? How does one become a successful friend, mother, teacher, lover, leader, or any one of the dozens of other starring and supporting roles that human beings are expected to play at various points in their lives?

Primarily, we all learn to function in various roles by emulating others whom we regard as being successful in those roles. We learn by doing what we have seen others do in particular situations and making adjustments in our future behaviors based on trial, error, and reflection. When we experience a new role for the first few times, we have to be content with role playing what we think a competent person would do in that particular role in that particular situation. This role play is based on a number of factors, including how we have seen others act in similar situations or what others whom we respect (parents, friends, mentors, and teachers) have told us is the proper or accepted way to act. It makes little difference what the role is: it can be anything from teaching to parenting to leading to making love. What's intriguing is that we can never be competent in any role as long as we are role playing. It's only after we experience a meta-morphosis and truly become that which we have been role playing (teacher, parent, leader, or lover) that we can reach our potential in a particular role.

Take learning to dance, for example. When we first learn to dance, we are certainly not dancers—in fact, most of us are more like unidentified bumbling objects than dancers! Even learning something as simple as the box step is a considerable challenge for some of us. As neophytes, we watch the instructor demonstrate how to complete the box step by performing four simple movements with the feet. It looks so smooth and easy when the instructor does it. Then when it's our turn to imitate the instructor's movements, it's not as simple as it first appeared. Because we are inexperienced and therefore vulnerable, most of us are ill at ease and self-conscious in this situation. We watch our feet, willing them to go in the right direction. All the while, we are counting to four over and over in our heads and trying to coordinate our awkward and clumsy steps with the beat of the music.

After a time, we are ready to partner up with the instructor and move in tandem to the music. We discover that this moving together with a dance partner to the music and counting to four over and over in our heads while doing the box step is a good deal more difficult than doing these things by oneself. Typically, most of us, while we are still beginners, get out of sync with the music. Sometimes we even trip over our own feet or, worse yet, we step on the toes of our partners.

Fortunately, with enough time, practice, and patience, we can stop counting "one, two, three, and four" over and over in our heads as we realize that this pattern never varies. With some additional practice, we are usually able to stop staring at our feet as we become convinced that our feet can complete a simple box without our constant visual scrutiny, and we are comfortable in the knowledge that our feet aren't going to run off and hide somewhere. This is a real breakthrough on the path to becoming a dancer, because once we are able to stop counting to four while intensely supervising our feet, we are able to look at our partners, carry on a simple conversation, smile occasionally, and even listen to and enjoy the music. With enough time and practice, we can even begin to innovate—to move out of the box, to turn in a circle, even to twirl our partners around. The point is that you can't *be* a dancer as long as you are watching your feet and counting your steps—you can only *do* dancing. With enough time and practice, however, most of us are able to stop thinking about what we are doing, relax, and enjoy the experience and, eventually, even begin to innovate. It is precisely at this point, when innovation begins, that we stop *doing* dancing and *become* dancers.

Leadership is a lot like dancing in this important respect. As long as we are role playing being a leader, asking ourselves questions such as "What do the textbooks say?" or "What would some other leader do in this particular situation or set of circumstances?" we can never be leaders; we can only do leadership. We don't become leaders until we can trust ourselves enough to listen to our inner voices and know for certain that these voices will guide us in making the decisions that we instinctively know are right for us as leaders. Bennis (1992) says that becoming a leader is synonymous with becoming yourself. In his view, "Leadership is first being, then doing. Everything the leader does reflects what he or she is" (p. 141). In other words, one can't do leadership; one must be a leader. And becoming a leader is a process of evolution that is a by-product of a person living his or her life in a particular way. As Bennis notes,

> No leader sets out to be a leader. People set out to live their lives, expressing themselves fully. When that expression is of value they become leaders. The point is to become yourself, to use yourself completely—all your skills, gifts, and energies—in order to make your vision manifest. You must withhold nothing. Become the person you started out to be, and enjoy the process of becoming. (pp. 111–112)

I agree with Bennis and all those others who insist that leadership is much more concerned with being than it is with doing. When I first had the opportunity to serve in a formal leadership role, I mistakenly believed that knowing how to do a lot of things well was the key to my success as a leader. I felt that I needed to display a great deal of expert power in order to meet the expectations of those whom I supervised. I was quite sure that I would be expected by my constituents to possess the knowledge and skills required to be the final authority in all matters great and small—to have the answers to all the questions. I now know that I couldn't have been more mistaken.

Although a broad knowledge of the operation one is expected to lead and a set of well-developed skills in how to get things done are clearly valuable assets for any leader, they aren't the crucial factors that determine success or failure in a leadership role. Knowledge and skills are prerequisites for assuming a leadership role in that they get you in the door, but they aren't the final arbiters of success. Who an individual is as a human being and a leader is far more important than how much he or she knows, or the set of skills he or she possesses. People choose to follow leaders not because of what they know, say, or do, but because they can readily identify with the leader's core values.

Leaders earn the trust and respect of their followers to the extent that they are able to demonstrate their allegiance to a set of widely accepted values as they carry out their daily responsibilities in a leadership role. The leader's actions in the role of leader serve as the confirmation that, as Sergiovanni (1992) has suggested, join the head, the heart, and the hand of leadership thereby making the leader authentic, or as I prefer to call it, *congruent.* The knowledge and skills required in order to develop a budget, hire and assign staff, plan and implement a curriculum, and so forth are not adequate substitutes for authenticity or congruency, which are manifested in characteristics such as honesty, integrity, caring, and commitment to a set of widely accepted values.

My personal life goal as a leader and a human being is to become more congruent. Let me explain what I mean by *congruent* through the use of a concept from geometry. According to my memory of what I was taught in Miss Spencer's ninth-grade geometry class, congruent triangles are identical. The three sides as well as the three angles in congruent triangles are all equal. If one were to place one congruent triangle on top of another, the first would cover the second completely, and no overlapping areas would remain. Therefore, my goal is to align the roles in my life so that they are like congruent triangles. In other words, I want the leader I am striving to be, and the person that I am, to essentially be one and the same.

It is clear to me that if I am to be successful in becoming more congruent in all aspects of my life, then I must strive to make the person I am on the outside identical to the person that I am on the inside, and vice versa. Cashman (1998) has offered this explanation of what it means to be congruent:

> What is required is a commitment to discover purpose and to grow to a new level of potential and expression. The same principles for leading apply to us in all areas of our life—family, community, business, ourselves— it's all about living our life congruent with our principles, beliefs, and character. (p. 68)

If I am truly congruent, then all the things that I believe or say or do will be consistent internally and externally. The people with whom I come into contact will never have to guess what I really mean or what I really think. My words and actions will be entirely consistent with my feelings and my beliefs. I will no longer be required to pretend, and I will never have to be concerned about using or manipulating others, because there will be no need to practice gamesmanship. Perhaps most important, I can become the person and the leader that I really want to be rather than constantly struggling to become the person and leader that others expect me to be. C. Michael Thompson, in his book, *The Congruent Life* (2000), emphasizes the importance of searching for the person that is you, so that you can become congruent, even if others perceive your search to be unreasonable:

> George Bernard Shaw once said that while the reasonable man adapts to the world, the unreasonable one persists in trying to make the world adapt to him. Thus he concluded, all progress depends on the unreasonable man. By that standard, we should all be unreasonable men and women. . . . If we have deep values, if we have vibrant beliefs dying to

find life in what we do for a living, if we yearn for the Congruent Life—then we should insist that the world conform itself to us. (p. 269)

I have no illusions about the difficulty of the goal I have set for myself. The world doesn't easily adapt to the individual, and I have already stumbled and even fallen occasionally on my personal journey toward congruency. However, I am convinced that the reward is worth the struggle, and I have a personal plan to help me accomplish my goal. Below I have outlined the major aspects in my plan. I invite you to adapt the steps that work for you and discard the rest.

1. *Embrace the notion that developing a loving relationship with myself is a* primary *life goal.* I can't begin to care for and serve others unless I have come to terms with who I am as a human being and have embraced that person in a loving and caring way. I must remember to always treat myself as I would a best friend so that I can have the capacity to give the support and encouragement to others that I have already given to myself.

2. *Accept the fact that becoming the person and the leader that I want to be is a never-ending journey.* Perfection is always an illusion. While I want to move toward perfection, I know that perfection is not a place, but a journey. I worked at a resort on the Maine coast one summer during my college years, and received perhaps some of the best advice anyone's ever given me. Madame Fortier, a guest at the hotel, said, "Never try to be the best, Leonard; it costs too much. Just try to be very good!" In other words, one should strive to live a balanced life and forget about perfection.

3. *Define and prioritize my values.* I can never reach my potential as a human being or a leader unless I know what I value most in my life. If I know the things that I value above all others, then I can be consistent as a leader and a person when I find myself engulfed in those "crucibles of character" that Badaracco (1997) has described so vividly.

4. *Practice becoming the person I want to be until that person becomes me.* I have frequently advised young people who are just starting out in their leadership careers to find a leader whom they greatly admire so that the chosen leader can be a role model and a mentor for them. I suggest that they study this special leader in her or his dealings with others and to emulate those positive characteristics and qualities that make that leader special. I tell them that even if a particular skill or quality feels unnatural at first, they should continue to practice until they are comfortable with it. A good golf swing is the most unnatural sensation imaginable to a novice golfer, but unless the novice golfer continues to practice that uncomfortable and unnatural swing until it becomes

natural and comfortable, he or she can never expect to master the game. The same is true about the basics of good leadership.

5. *Emphasize doing what's right rather than not doing what's wrong.* Several months ago, I was relaxing in the Jacuzzi at a local fitness center after exercising. Two other men were having a conversation about how unfair "the system" was to white men in general. They both agreed that people of color got all the breaks, all the good job opportunities, and so on, while white men were vilified and even punished for sins of past generations. The conversation got more and more ridiculous, but I resisted the urge to take exception. In truth, it would have been uncomfortable for me to express my views that were diametrically opposed to what I was hearing. Eventually, I exited the Jacuzzi, showered, and went back to work. It was only later that I thought, "You know you condoned what those two men were saying by not taking exception. While you didn't do wrong by joining in the conversation and supporting their views, you also didn't do right by expressing another point of view." Not doing what is wrong is not enough for a leader. Leadership requires one to do what is right, even when it is difficult or uncomfortable to do so.

6. *Remember that the only real joy in life is the result of serving others.* There are many intrinsic and extrinsic rewards that accrue to those in leadership roles, and these rewards can be distracting and even dangerous to leaders. Caring leadership requires those who lead to remember that they have been given a great gift by those who have trusted them to lead and that faithful, committed service is the only way to repay the gift they have been given. All the rewards that come with leadership are temporary and transitory except for the knowledge that your leadership has contributed substantially to the lives of people and organizations that you have served.

7. *Find comfort in the knowledge that the more you struggle, the more you are serving.* Heifetz and Linsky (2002) have reminded us that, not only are there wonderful rewards associated with leadership, there are also significant costs associated with leadership. Caring leadership requires moving people out of their comfort zones, making difficult decisions, saying "No" to people you care about when you wish you could say "Yes." I had a friend who once served on the state board of education in our state who told me that she was so distressed by the infighting, the politics, and the "stupid decisions" that typified the board that she couldn't sleep after a meeting. I told her that she should feel great because the fact that she struggled so much to serve in this role should confirm for her how much she was needed on the board and what a significant contribution she was making in her role as a board member. I tell young people who are starting out in leadership roles

that, if being in a leadership role always feels good to you, then you probably aren't doing it right!

8. *Go up on the balcony and down in the basement from time to time and observe the dance.* To be a caring leader, you can't just care about your own area of responsibility, your people, your piece of the organization; you also have to care about the total organization and all the people that comprise the organization. You and those for whom you are directly responsible can never be winners while the organization loses. If a quarterback throws six touchdown passes and the team loses, the quarterback doesn't win because he performed well while some other aspects of the team performed poorly. The quarterback loses, too! Caring leaders care about the total organization. They stay in close touch with those above them and those below them in the organizational structure and do everything in their power to understand the role that others play in order to support them and to help them succeed so that everyone can win together.

9. *Never forget that motive means everything for those who lead.* Why a leader does something is far more important than what she or he does. We are all familiar with the old expression, "Managers do things right while leaders do the right things." While I believe that good leaders also do things right, I firmly believe that people follow leaders not because of what they know, say, or do, but because they identify with who the leader is as a human being. People follow leaders because they admire, respect, and agree with the values that are reflected in the thoughts, deeds, and actions of leaders in the workplace. Furthermore, I believe that because caring leaders have pure, other-oriented motives guiding their actions, they have the capacity to fail from time to time and still be lifted up, admired, and respected by those they serve. Trust me, uncaring leaders never have that kind of insurance.

10. *Maintain an optimistic and grateful attitude.* Leaders must be positive, optimistic, confident people. Life is a series of ups and downs for everyone. We will all suffer our share of wins and losses. When I'm down, I have to remember that the wins will come if I can be consistent and persistent in my efforts. When I am up, I have to appreciate and enjoy the moment while also realizing that the good feelings won't last forever. Life is about losing and gaining things at the same time. We can't spend our time and energy regretting the things that we may have lost. We have to be grateful for the things that we were fortunate enough to have had and for the things that may come to us again in the future.

11. *Remember that significant growth can't happen without reflection.* Like it or not, most of what we learn in life is the result of trial and error.

We all have to make our share of mistakes in order to grow. But if we want to derive the maximum growth from our mistakes as well as our successes, we must actively engage in reflection. If we don't actively engage in reflection, then we will be like that fellow I mentioned earlier who has one year of experience twenty-five times, and we won't grow much at all. There are many good ways for leaders to reflect. Of course, the most obvious way to reflect is simply to regularly set aside some time to think about who you are, what you are doing, and where you want to go in your life. Another very effective way to reflect is to regularly write in a journal, chronicling your thoughts, decisions, and actions while comparing these to the results expected and the results achieved. A third good way to reflect is to ask for feedback from those who are close to you and whose opinions you respect. A fourth way is to survey those whom you serve about your effectiveness as a leader using one of the many good instruments available for this purpose. The important thing is not how leaders reflect, but that they do it. As Cashman (1998) has suggested,

> Take some time to observe your own behavior. Is it coming from a place of purpose? Is it releasing energy, or is it coming from a place of obligation, conditioning, duty, and bondage? Has your life become a series of "have to do's" or is it moving in the direction of "want to do's"? (p. 73)

Reflection is the best way that caring leaders have at their disposal to profit from their experiences and move along the path they have chosen to become the best and most congruent leaders that they can be.

Although I will never reach my ultimate destination as a leader, I plan to take as many steps along the path toward that destination as I possibly can. With every new day, I want the people in my life to feel that they can trust my leadership a little more than they could the day before as they witness the consistency of the person I say I am as a leader with the deeds that I perform in the name of leadership. I don't care how many sides or angles ultimately define the shape of my life as long as the internal and external manifestations of who I am are congruent.

How about you? Can you force yourself to break out of that tight little box step that limits your ability to lead? Can you trust yourself enough to find your own leadership style, to experiment with your own patterns and your own rhythms? Are you secure enough to be that "unreasonable man or woman" who is an innovator and a risk taker as you wrestle with the problems of leadership? Can you feel confident enough to stop counting your steps and to resist the urge to constantly stare at your feet? Will you allow yourself the freedom to turn and twist and twirl as the spirit moves you? Do you accept the responsibility to trust your instincts and serve as your own choreographer in this peculiar dance we call leadership? Can you relax and begin to enjoy the challenges of providing leadership for those who have trusted you to lead? If someone should ask you, can you tell them why you are on your way to "visit Bob"? Finally, can you frame answers that satisfy you as a leader and a human being for most, if not all, the critical questions that have been posed for leaders in this book?

If you can come to the realization that you can do all these things, then, at that precise moment, you will be dancing the dance of a leader. You will stop doing leadership, and you will become the leader that you want to be! Don't worry about stepping on a few toes here and there as you dance your dance as a leader. Just remember, you're the choreographer! Only you and you alone can dance this unique and wonderful dance. Upon reflection, you will find that any missteps you make will simply serve as signposts to point you in the right direction. Good luck, and remember to relax and enjoy the music!

REFERENCES

Anderson, L., Cook, N., Pellicer, L., Sears, J., & Spradling, R. (1989). *A study of EIA-funded remedial and compensatory programs in South Carolina.* Columbia, SC: South Carolina Educational Policy Center.

Autry, J. (1991). *Love and profit: The art of caring leadership.* New York: Morrow.

Badaracco, J. L., Jr. (1997). *Defining moments: When managers must choose between right and right.* Boston: Harvard Business School Press.

Bennis, W. G. (1992). *On becoming a leader.* New York: Addison-Wesley.

Bennis, W. G., & Goldsmith, J. (2003). *Learning to lead: A workbook on becoming a leader.* New York: Basic Books.

Bennis, W. G., & Thomas, R. J. (2002). *Geeks and geezers: How era, values, and defining moment shape leaders.* Boston: Harvard Business School Press.

Best Employers in Canada. (2007). Best Employers in Canada Study. http://was7 .hewitt.com/bestemployers/canada/best.htm.

Blanchard, K., & Hodges, P. (2003). *The servant leader.* Minneapolis, MN: J. Countryman.

Blanchard, K., & O'Connor, M. (1997). *Managing by values.* San Francisco: Berrett-Koehler.

Block, P. (1993). *Stewardship: Choosing service over self-interest.* San Francisco: Berrett-Koehler.

Bolman, L., & Deal, T. (1995). *Leading with soul: An uncommon journey of spirit.* San Francisco: Jossey-Bass.

Bracey, H., Rosenblum, J., Sanford, A., & Trueblood, R. (1990). *Managing from the heart.* New York: Dell.

Brooks, J. L. (Producer), & Scott, T. (Director). (1996). *Jerry Maguire* [Motion picture]. Culver City, CA: Tristar.

Buckingham, M., & Coffman, C. (1999). *First break all the rules: What the world's greatest managers do differently.* New York: Simon & Schuster.

Burns, J. M. (1978). *Leadership.* New York: Harper & Row.

Cashman, K. (1998). *Leadership from the inside out.* Minneapolis, MN: TLGC.

Charnin, M. (1977). *Annie.* Milwaukee, WI: Hal Leonard.

Coffman, C., & Gonzalez-Molina, G. (2002). *Follow this path: How the world's greatest organizations drive growth by unleashing human potential.* New York: Warner Books.

Collins, J. (2001). *Good to great.* New York: HarperCollins.

Csikszentmihalyi, M. (2003). *Good business: Leadership, flow, and the making of meaning.* New York: Penguin Books.

De Pree, M. (1989). *Leadership is an art.* New York: Bantam Doubleday

Fussman, C. (2004). What I've learned: The heavyweights. *Esquire, 141*(1), 88

Goleman, D., Boyatzis, R., & McKee, A. (2002) *Primal leadership: Realizing the power of emotional intelligence.* Boston: Harvard Business School Press.

Greenleaf, R. K. (1977). *Servant leadership: A journey into the nature of legitimate power and greatness.* New York: Paulist Press.

Greenleaf, R. K. (1996). *On becoming a servant leader.* San Francisco: Jossey-Bass.

Handy, C. (1989). *The age of unreason.* Boston: Harvard Business School Press.

Heifetz, R. A. (1994). *Leadership without easy answers.* Cambridge, MA: Belnap Press of Harvard University.

Heifetz, R. A., Linsky, M. (2002). *Leadership on the line.* Boston: Harvard Business School Press.

Hogan, R., Curphy, G. J., & Hogan, J. (1994). What we know about leadership: Effectiveness and personality. *American Psychologist, 49,* 493–504.

Howe, C. (2003). What makes an organization a great place to work? *Employee Benefits Journal, 28*(2), 41–43.

Johnson, C. (2005). *Meeting the ethical challenges of leadership.* Thousand Oaks, CA: Sage.

Kahn, W. (1990). Psychological conditions of personal engagement and disengagement at work. *Academy of Management Journal, 33*(4), 692–724.

Kouzes, J., & Posner, B. (1995). *The leadership challenge: How to keep getting extraordinary things done in organizations.* San Francisco: Jossey-Bass Publishers.

Kouzes, J., & Posner, B. (1999). *Encouraging the heart: A leader's guide to rewarding and recognizing others.* San Francisco: Jossey-Bass Publishers.

Loehr, J., & Schwartz, T. (2003). *The power of full engagement.* New York: Free Press (Simon & Schuster).

Reichheld, F. F. (1996). *The loyalty effect: The hidden force behind growth, profits, and lasting value.* Boston: Harvard Business School Press.

Sanford, B. (2002a). The high cost of disengaged employees. *Gallup Management Journal Online,* 1–2. http://www.gallupjournal.com/CA/ee/20020415.asp.

Sanford, B. (2002b). Building a highly engaged workforce. *Gallup Management Journal Online,* 1–3. http://www.gallupjournal.com/CA/ee/20020603.asp.

Sanford, B. (2003). Driving performance in the emotional economy. *Gallup Management Journal Online,* 1–4. http://www.gallupjournal.com.

Senge, P. (1990). *The fifth discipline: The art of the learning organization.* New York: Doubleday.

Sergiovanni, T. J. (1992). *Moral leadership: Getting to the heart of school improvement.* San Francisco: Jossey-Bass.

Simpson, D., & Bruckheimer, J. (Producers), & Scott, T. (Director). (1993). *Top gun* [Motion picture]. Hollywood: Paramount.

Smith, J. D. (2003). *In search of better angels: Stories of disability in the human family.* Thousand Oaks, CA: Corwin Press.

Solomon, R. C. (1992). *Ethics and excellence: Cooperation and integrity in business.* New York: Oxford University Press.

Stanford-Blair, N., & Dickmann, M. H. (2005). *Leading coherently: Reflections from leaders around the world.* Thousand Oaks, CA: Sage.

Suters, E. (1991). Stew Leonard: Soul of a leader. *Executive Excellence, 8*(6), 13–14.

Thamara, T. (1994). Comment: At CB&T, culture of caring yields consistent profits. *American Banker, 159,* 19.

Thompson, C. M. (2000). *The congruent life: Following the inward path to fulfilling work and inspired leadership.* San Francisco: Jossey-Bass.

Vaill, P. (1989). *Managing as a performing art: New ideas for a world of chaotic change.* San Francisco: Jossey-Bass.

Welch, J. (2005). *Winning.* New York: HarperCollins.

Wheatley, M. J. (1992). *Leadership and the new science: Learning about organization from an orderly universe.* San Francisco: Berrett-Koehler.

Wheatley, M. J. (2005). *Finding our way: Leadership for an uncertain time.* San Francisco: Berrett-Koehler.

Yudd, R. (2002). Model behavior: Success very often follows leaders who can practice what they preach. *Nation's Restaurant News, 36*(25), 44, 168.

INDEX

Acknowledging the contributions
 of others, 138–139
Aging, 152

Balanced life, 148
Behavioral theorists, 14
Beliefs about people, 44–47, 51
Bennis, Warren, 136–137, 139, 162–163
Best friend, 107–108, 144–150
Burns, James MacGregor, 20–21

Campbell, Joseph, viii
Cares, self-assessments about, 35, 41–42
Caring
 demanding nature of, 149
 description of, 35
 employee engagement and, 31, 34
 examples of, 19–20
 financial success, 36–37
 importance of, 16–17, 20
 lack of, 36
 leadership and, 31–32
 leader's reason for caring about, 33–34
 organization and, 167
 organization building and, 33
 purpose and, 35
 work, 26
 wrong things, 36–37
 for yourself, 147–150, 165
Caring organizations, 127
Change, 90, 156–157
Climate of organization, 32
Coffman, Curt, 29–31
Compensatory education, 120–124
Congruent, 163–164
Connectedness, in organizations, 126
Contingency leadership theory, 14

Control, 43–44
Core values, 36
Crises, 149
Criticism, 92, 144–146
Crucibles of character, 75
Cultural norms, in U.S. society, 145
Cynics, 37–38, 46–47

Decision(s)
 daily amount of, 80
 outcomes of, 99–102
 right versus right, 102–103
Decision making
 assertion of authority through, 81, 83–84
 description of, 64
 dilemmas in, 102–103, 153, 166
 involvement in, 70
 middle ground in, 99–100
 motives for, 80–85
 safe approach to, 90–91
 self-assessments, 81–85
 vignette about, 64–70
Defining moments, 75, 103
De Pree, Max, 15, 46, 141
Dreams, 160–161
Drucker, Peter, vii

Education Improvement Act, 121
Egalitarian leadership, 56
Employee(s). *See also* People
 acknowledging the contributions of, 138
 caring by, 41
 disengagement of, 31
Employee engagement
 caring and, 31, 34
 definition of, 27
 effort and, correlation between, 29

employer practices that promote, 28
level of, 29–30
productivity and, 30–31, 33
Employer, 28
Emulation, 161, 165

Failure, 147
Feedback, 168
Financial success, caring about, 36–37
First-year teachers, 59–60, 62
Flow, in organization, 41
Followers
    consent by, 20
    description of, 15
    leader's responsibility to, 97, 136–143
    sense of purpose for, 137–138
    trust and respect of, 163
Forman, Michele, 17
Fragmenting of organizations, 139
Friendship, 144

Great man theory, 13

Handy, Charles, 35
Heifetz, Ron, vii
Hierarchies, 56
Honesty, 140, 142

Laughing, 148
Leader(s)
    assertion of authority by, 81, 83–84
    beliefs about people, 44–47
    caring by, 33–34
    characteristics of, 14–15
    congruent, 163–164
    control by, 43–44
    core values of, 36
    corporation performance affected by, 15
    costs of being, 130
    debts owed to followers, 139–140
    definition of, 22
    effectiveness of, 13
    effect on others, 22
    emulation of, 165
    evolution of becoming, 163
    honesty by, 140, 142
    importance of little things, 111–112
    integrity promotion by, 139
    mistakes by, 147

    motives of, 81–85, 167
    as observer, 153–154
    as participator, 153–154
    passionate, 38–41
    people-related issues for, 28
    purpose of, 150
    reason for becoming, 133–135
    responsibilities of, 4, 15, 75
    risk taking by, 87–91
    role playing as, 162
    roles of, 149
    safety in decision making by, 90–91
    school. *See* School leaders
    self-assessments by, 41, 85–86
    sharing of feelings by, 148–149
    strength of, 98
    superiority of, 97
    types of, 16
    universal struggles for, 158
    willful, 16
Leadership
    caring and, 31–32
    challenges associated with, 87–90, 92
    definition of, 13, 21–22
    difficulties associated with, 77–78
    egalitarian, 56
    employee engagement promoted by, 27–28
    granting of, 141
    human costs of, 78
    as a journey, 17–18
    meaning in life achieved
        through, 134
    methods of, 43–44
    moral, 19, 21
    passionate caring and, 38–39
    as process, 22
    purpose of, 97
    requirements for, 163
    rewards associated with, 166
    skills necessary for, 163
    teacher, 17
    traditional approach to, 65–66
    traits associated with, 17–18, 32
    trust and, 162
Leadership theories
    contingency, 14
    great man theory, 13
    history of, 13–22

situational, 14
trait theory, 14
Learning by doing, 161–162
Learning community, 126
Level 5 leaders, 16
Life
    as a journey, 9, 155–157, 165
    uncertainty of, 3
Life goals, 150, 155–157, 164
Little things
    attention to, 108–111
    leader's recognition of importance
        of, 111–112, 138
    success and, 107

Manager
    effectiveness of, 31–32
    employee engagement promotion
        by, 30–31
McGuire, Cynthia Cervantes, 17–19
McNamara, Robert, vii
Mentoring, 165
Mistakes, 147, 168
Moral leadership, 19, 21
Mother Teresa, 105
Motives, for decisions,
        80–85, 167

Noncaring, 36

Optimism, 141–142, 167
Organizations
    caring in, 41, 127
    climate of, 32
    connectedness in, 126–127
    employee engagement in, 27
    flow in, 41
    fragmenting of, 139
    hierarchies in, 56
    ideals for, 157
    invisible fields in, 123
    as a living system, 157
    moral leadership in, 19
    purpose of, 138
    reminding employees about what is
        important in, 139
    risk taking in, 90–91
    roles in, 55–56
    shared vision in, 126

support offered by, 50–51
values of, 139
as virtuous enterprises, 126–127

Passionate caring, 38–39
Passionate leaders
    example of, 39–41
    importance of, 39
People. *See also* Employee(s)
    beliefs about, 44–47, 51
    factors that influence, 46
    good job performed by, 46–47
    leader's beliefs about, 44–47
    passionate, 38–39
    personal personnel philosophy
        about, 46–47
    reminding about what is important, 139
    self-assessments on how you treat, 43
    stereotyped views of, 45
    support for, 46–51
Personal personnel philosophy, 46
Personal reflection, 152–156, 167–168
Philippines, 53–56, 62
Play, 148
Prejudice, 114–119
Prioritizing of values, 165
Problems, vii–viii
Productivity, 30–31, 33

Questions, knowing
    the answers to, 3–4

Racism, 114–119
Realistic optimism, 142
Redman, Peggy, vii
Reflection, 152–156, 167–168
Relaxation, 148
Respect of followers, 163
Responsibility
    assumption of, 72–75
    examples of, 75–78
    by leader, 75
    rewards of, 77–78
    self-assessments, 78
Right versus right decisions, 102–103
Risk taking
    assumption of, 91–92
    creativity and, 92
    criticism and, 92

encouraging of, 93
example of, 87–90, 92–93
by leaders, 87–91
in organizations, 90–91
power of, 92
rewards associated with, 93
success and, 91–92
Role playing, 161
Roles, 55–56

Sacred heart, 150
Sanford, Barb, 29
School
compensatory education, 120–124
jungle-like atmosphere in, 97
nurturing and caring
environment in, 97
studies of, 120–122
as virtuous enterprise, 126–128
School leaders, 40–41, 60, 62, 97
Self-assessments
decision-making motives, 81–85
by leaders, 41, 85–86
responsibility, 78
things you care about, 35, 41–42
Self-concept, 146
Self-criticism, 145–146
Self-enlightenment, 2–3
Self-growth, 167–168
Selfishness, 37
Self-love, 144, 165
Self-reflection, 152–156, 167–168
Self-sacrifice, 157
Self-talk, 146–148
Sense of purpose, 137–138
Servant leaders, 141
Service and serving, 141, 166
Shadowing forward, 103
Shared vision, 65, 126
Sharing of feelings, 148–149
Situational leadership theory, 14
Smith, J. David, 118
Society
competitive nature of, 145
cultural norm in, 145
Stereotyped views of people, 45
Strengths, 98, 148

Success
celebration of, 148
communicating of, 138
little things that matter, 107
risk taking and, 91–92
Superiority
of leaders, 97
lion metaphor of, 94–96
Support, 46–51

Taylor, Frederick, 14
Teacher
commitment by, 60, 65
difficulties for, 60
first-year, 59–60, 62
reason for becoming, 133–135
school leader's support for, 60, 62
traits of, 60–61
vignette about, 58–60
Teacher leadership, 17
Thomas, Robert J., 136
Thompson, C. Michael, 164
Thoughtful observers, 153
Thurber, James, 3
Tobin, Walt, 17
Trait theory, 14
Trust, 162–163
Trusting environments, 140–141

Vision
building of, 127
shared, 65, 126

Welch, Jack, 4, 21, 46, 50, 139
Wheatley, Margaret J., 3, 43–44,
123, 135, 143, 157
Willful leaders, 16
Work
active engagement in, 26
caring for, 26
employee engagement in, 27, 29
Work ethic, 107
Workplace
acknowledging contributions in, 138
leader's responsibilities, 26–27
Workshops, 2–3

Yelvington, Cecil, 24–25, 137

CORWIN
PRESS

The Corwin Press logo—a raven striding across an open book—represents the union of courage and learning. Corwin Press is committed to improving education for all learners by publishing books and other professional development resources for those serving the field of PreK–12 education. By providing practical, hands-on materials, Corwin Press continues to carry out the promise of its motto: **"Helping Educators Do Their Work Better."**